BOHEMIAN
VERSUS
BOURGEOIS

BOHEMIAN
VERSUS
BOURGEOIS

FRENCH SOCIETY AND THE
FRENCH MAN OF LETTERS
IN THE
NINETEENTH CENTURY

CÉSAR GRAÑA

BASIC BOOKS, INC.

Publishers

NEW YORK   LONDON

TO MICAELA ANDREA GRANA

ACKNOWLEDGMENTS

No BOOK, however personal, is written without the presence and concern of others. In reminding myself of this, I would like to make a number of acknowledgments.

The first goes to Prof. Reinhard Bendix, Department of Sociology, University of California. The resolve to undertake this book owes much to his trust that literary expression could be studied by a sociologist without selling short the integrity of literature or the demands of social analysis. He witnessed the beginnings of this work and followed its subsequent fortunes without sparing his critical caution or slackening his encouragement.

Prof. Leo Lowenthal, also of the Department of Sociology of the University of California, strengthened me in the belief that the social sciences and the humanities should not be politely alienated from each other, but naturally curious about their common interests. His many marks of support were always welcome.

I give my thanks also to Prof. Eugene Burdick, of the Department of Political Science at Berkeley, who gave warmly of his interest and time in reading the manuscript.

Seymour M. Lipset, professor of sociology and director of

the Institute of International Studies at the University of California, offered the kind of hearing without which the best of intellectual intentions might never see their reward.

I also want to offer recognition to the students in my course on the Sociology of Intellectual Life given at the University of California in the Summer of 1960. They were a memorable group—ardent, versatile, and precociously learned. The six weeks spent with them were a constantly refreshing dialogue, during which many of the concluding ideas of this book took their shape. Prof. Marc Galanter, of the University of Chicago offered, besides the abundance of his intellectual responsiveness, the sort of comradeship and hospitality which would be very difficult to repay.

I have nothing but gratitude for Marigay Graña and for Pauline Graña. With the dedication and the endurance of loyalty, they contributed those hours of tedious work without which no book can reach its completion.

The Department of Sociology of the University of California and a grant advanced by the friendly readiness of Dean Alan B. Simpson of the College of the University of Chicago made possible the final preparation of the manuscript.

CÉSAR GRAÑA

February 1964

INTRODUCTION

THE FIRST PRINCIPLE of any sociological analysis of a literary period is easy to state; such analysis must be guided by the social content and intention of literature itself. In some cases a writer's social sentiments are openly on view. In others they have to be unveiled and sorted out. Some writers must be read as reporters of a given social scene; they deal with the "facts" of speech, manner, attitude, and atmosphere as these are re-created by the literary imagination. Others are more "sociological." Their aim is the objective exposure of economic forces and social relations and the way in which these direct the actions of individuals. Some forms of literature are intended as social propaganda, while others fastidiously avoid any explicit social meaning. Yet even in this latter case, the tastes which an author chooses to nurse or scorn are a testimony to what he feels he owes the social order.

If the social intentions or implications of literature can take different forms, it is also true that the sociological critic of literature is never the servant of one perspective alone. He may look at the content of a book, the life history of the writer, or the connection between the two. Or he may look at literature as a profession, with a given relationship to institutions, the state, social classes, or the public.* He is also entitled to a concern with style, for style, whether good or bad, can convey some of the essential features of a writer's image of social experience. For example, one of the most "Kafkaesque" elements in Kafka's novels is his use of certain stage effects. Lighting is always poor, making it difficult for one character to know the age, identity or appearance of another until the two come very close. And speeches, which begin meaningfully, descend first into bemusing and then into tormenting nonsense. In *The Trial*, K, the accused, is at first able to comprehend the judge's words, but after a few minutes, he must strain. Finally, the judge's recitation of the charges begins to reach him in rising portentous and distorted wafts of sound, while K stands in the chamber (where is not clear) humbled and mystified.[1] In *The Castle*, the novel begins with the arrival of the main character at a village from which he attempts to communicate by telephone with the authorities who reside at a nearby castle and who have summoned him for some unstated purpose. But these communications always break down when connections go bad and voices become garbled or some important person becomes petulantly incoherent at the other end of the line.[2] Both these devices, light and sound, are indispensable to the creation of Kafka's world, a world in which every act and every fact seem to be adrift in enormous ambivalences, echoes, and intimations.

In a similar way, Stendhal's determination to write instantaneously, in order to avoid self-deception or a literary and

---

* The recognition of these alternatives and of the link that often exists among them should be enough to ease the fear that the sociological analyst always subjects literature to the same raw measurements and the same thick-fingered handling. As for the presumed conflict between art and the sociological method and the belief that one cannot look for social meaning without soiling the face of beauty, the answer seems plain and undramatic. W. H. Auden has said that social history may explain why Shakespeare's poetry is different from Browning's, but not why it is better. That is to say that sociologists of the arts are not aesthetic critics nor have to be. And we may add that this is far from an unfortunate situation, since art with explicit social intention is often bad art.

aesthetic unity not true to the facts, is also a part of his method
of understanding social events. Speaking of Napoléon Bonaparte
in his *History of the Restoration,* the poet and historian Lamartine condemned the emperor for his corruption of French na-
tionalism and his exploitation of the best in the public passions
of his time. Lamartine had nothing good to say about Napoléon
as a ruler or as a man. But he admired him as a writer because,
he said, his prose is true to experience, the other side, as it were,
of the events themselves. This, in Lamartine's opinion, made
Napoléon the greatest reporter of human doings since Machiavelli.[3] As for Stendhal, he admired Napoléon above all other
men as a social and psychological creature; his own view, of society as a battlefield and of personal etiquette as strategy, can
adequately be called "social Bonapartism." We should not be
surprised, therefore, to find that Stendhal's style appeared to
André Gide as Napoléon's appeared to Lamartine.

With Stendhal one sentence never calls into being or is produced
by what went on before. Each stands perpendicular to the fact or
the idea.[4]

In a recent essay on the place of the intellectual in the United
States, Marcus Cunliffe worried that he might be contributing
nothing more than another instance of the literary phenomenon
he calls *The Article.* He says:

I can imagine a Western writer, over the last thirty years, being
able to place *The Article* in any of a score of periodicals, under
any of a dozen titles, with or without the qualification of American
that appears in mine. "The Role/Problem/Fate/Dilemma/Plight/
Isolation/Alienation of the Individual/Intellectual/Writer/Poet/Art-
ist:" Any of these alternatives would do with appropriate minor
alterations in the text.[5]

The subject of Cunliffe's concern is also the subject of this book.
However, I propose to show that, if not *The Article,* certainly
The Problem has existed for a much longer period than Cunliffe
assigns to it and that the "outsiders," marginal and even "invisible" men of modern literature,* have been endemic in Western

culture, not for thirty but for one hundred and thirty years; so have the social realities of which they are a symptom.

One sometimes hears that the ailments of literary loneliness are already present in the lives or works of Shakespeare, Dante, or Socrates. But this can only be said by neglecting the specific content of different forms of isolation and suffering. It is true, for example, that Hamlet is alone, but it is also true that he lives in a world of mothers and fathers, of kings and princes with their passions and duties. What outrages him is the violation of the moral code of that world, and he could never be called an alienated man in the modern sense, because he is not the creature without the sense of social membership implied in the term. Dante felt bitter about having to climb the stairways of the powerful, but he was also literary executor of the highest spiritual ideals of the Middle Ages. And the point of Socrates' tragedy is certainly that it was caused by a loyalty to Athenian social traditions greater than that of his enemies.

It is likely that there has always been some sort of strain between the self-conscious observer of social reality and the vested interests of the society—cultural, moral, and economic. But, when we speak of modern literary discontent, we speak of something far more extreme and profound, as social feeling, than any melancholy of the past and of something far more widespread, which reaches beyond the practicing intellectual to those innumerable persons who regard themselves as sensitive or creative. Modern literary irritability and gloom turns from one dominant social force to another: democracy, vulgarity, industrialization, or all at the same time. Early in the nineteenth cen-

---

* Those who read H. G. Wells' *The Invisible Man* only as a science-fiction horror may not have noticed the *ressentiment* of the main character, his social suspicions and rages, his contempt for the common people, his disgust with commercial civilization, and the hatred of his own physical peculiarities; he is an albino. In Ralph Ellison's novel, similarly entitled *Invisible Man,* this last is given a complex sociological reversal. The protagonist is a Negro who disappears as an individual because whites cannot see him as separate from the collective Black.

tury Alfred de Musset wrote: "Damned Be the Family, and Society. Cursed Be the Home and Cursed Be the City. Damnation upon the Motherland." In what other period of history can we find such immediately felt personal contempt and bitterness thrown at such large and imposing targets?

"Alienation" has become an intellectual folk term. But, curiously, the vividness with which it is felt seems to obscure any definite explanation of its sources. To overcome this obscurity is one of the purposes of this book. Its first section is a documented case history of the social conditions surrounding literature in one country, France, during a certain period of the nineteenth century. The second is an account of the ideas of three writers—Stendhal, Flaubert, and Baudelaire—who, speaking from their particular experience of French society, extended their vision to an analysis of modern life and the relation of the literary artist to it. The third is a recapitulation of those themes of literary discontent which link the beginnings of that discontent in the nineteenth century with the literature of the present.

I chose France during the middle portion of the nineteenth century—roughly the reign of Louis Philippe of Orléans—because it offered the clearest example of the arrival and establishment of certain social facts which are the condition or target of so much modern literary unhappiness: the disappearance of the traditional forms of literary sponsorship, the final emergence of the middle class as the dominant class, not only economically but politically and ideologically, and the advent of industrialization, technology, popular government, social utilitarianism, the concentration of cultural life in the cities, and intellectual unemployment. Of course, these social and economic happenings do not alone explain everything. Romantic ennui, the theory of personal genius, and other badges of the period, had begun years before. But it is at this time that the folkways of literary defiance of modern culture and the tradition of unresolvable tension between society and the man of letters become visibly entrenched.

The peculiarities that a specific time and place give to a social problem do not always obscure its general outlines. In fact, the opposite may be true. We may grant Paris all of its splendor and volubility as a cultural arena and still view it as an example of the big city as mover and exploiter of modern culture. Indeed, a situation may be taken as representative because of the very idiosyncrasy of its features. The destruction of the traditional state and aristocracy and the rise of modern political agitation created a cultural crisis throughout modern Europe. In France, however, these events occurred with a suddenness giving them an almost theatrical intensity and character. And it can happen that a historical event is so radically novel that even its elementary manifestations will challenge witnesses to foresee many of its future implications. For instance, France did not industrialize so quickly or so widely as England. But we still recognize what Flaubert says about industrialization as either true of some of the consequences of modern production or true of the literary view of it. If ideas were merely echoes of social reality, there would be no great need to study them; facts alone would be enough. But, in fact, they are versions of reality which may even create the styles of intellectual response. Stendhal, Flaubert, or Baudelaire are not only writers of the French scene. What they said raised nearly every issue of the still-running debate of modern culture generally. They also contributed to the invention of characteristic forms of despair, defiance, attack, and escape which comprise the language of literary discontent.

The concluding portion avails itself of European and American novels, essays, plays, and criticism; its aim is to document the history of literary assaults on modern society over a wide range of themes and imagery. Before doing this, however, a prototype profile of the modern literary *malaise* was needed, and I found it in the verdict of contemporary culture given by Stendhal, Flaubert, and Baudelaire. For this I used only letters, journals, and incidental writings, leaving out poetry and fiction. For such a restriction I can only claim one advantage—the comfort it afforded in dealing with overt statements of social sentiment

and observation. I chose these statements, not because they were
more eloquent or artistically memorable, but because they were
unmistakable.

NOTES TO THE INTRODUCTION

1. Franz Kafka, *The Trial,* trans. Edwin & Willa Muir (New York:
Alfred A. Knopf, 1941).

2. Franz Kafka, *The Castle,* introduction by Thomas Mann, trans.
Edwin & Willa Muir (New York: Alfred A. Knopf, 1944).

3. Alphonse de Lamartine, *The History of the Restoration of the
Monarchy in France* (4 vols.; New York: Harper and Brothers, 1851), **I,**
247.

4. André Gide, *The Counterfeiters with the Journal of the Counterfeiters* (New York: Alfred A. Knopf, 1959), p. 382.

5. Marcus Cunliffe, "The American Intellectual," *Encounter,* May,
1955, p. 23.

CONTENTS

Contents

BOHEMIAN
VERSUS
BOURGEOIS

Part I

The Social World
of
Modern French Letters

CHAPTER I

THE MONARCHY OF
THE MIDDLE CLASSES:
FRANCE 1830-1848

ON THE EVE of the French Revolution the Abbé Sieyès asked "What is the Third Estate?" and answered his own question by saying that it was "everything." It is clear that Sieyès intended this as a political slogan, meaning that the middle class was the most productive and, therefore, the most deserving of all classes. But his question forecasts an obstinate sociological problem: what *is* the middle class and what can be put within it?

The point has been argued across intellectual distances from Karl Marx to D. H. Lawrence, and its history includes descriptions, praises, and accusations of the middle class by innumerable European and American historians, critics, and sociologists. In the case of France, however, the history of the middle class, at least until the Revolution of 1789, shows that, although cultural differences existed within it, there was also a customary consensus about its occupational character. The French bourgeoisie was affluent, but cautious. It accumulated possessions, but it avoided economic risks, seeking instead security, well-being, and an elegant way of life. As the middle class has historically done, the French bourgeoisie advanced itself by education and brainwork. Furthermore, the royal bureaucracy of pre-revolutionary France provided opportunities and rewards for both and thus brought the bourgeoisie into a system which combined public service with public honors. This same system also brought the French magistrate closer to the courtier and the nobleman, that is to say, to that social world whose standards of taste were regarded by all aspiring persons as the model of a cultured existence. Hence an important segment of the bourgeoisie obeyed those essentially aristocratic distinctions of cultural and spiritual style that dominated French life until the end of the Old Regime. It was one thing, therefore, to belong to a shopkeeping, trading, or manufacturing family, living by the market day after day and another to be a member of an upper bourgeois household and have as one's goal a finely mannered life supported by governmental posts or investment returns.[1]

This is not to say that one does not find in pre-revolutionary France, as in England, homiletic literary eulogies of the hardworking burgher, his abstinence from waste and luxury and his tireless promotion of the family fortunes. Such literature exists, just as whole branches of the bourgeoisie remained faithfully and proudly attached to the code of industriousness. In many cases, however, as has been true of other societies, it is clear that manner and style quickly followed a successful family history of monetary intake. Erich Auerbach has documented the preciousness with which segments of the bourgeoisie echoed the mandates of upper-class etiquette, and the self-conscious royalist fawning of the merchants in the luxury trade. Already in early seventeenth-century plays we find such figures as the enriched businessman who, taking a visitor on a tour of his choice new furnishings, says to him:

Admirez ce bon lit et l'accompagnement,
Ces pliants, ces fauteils, les broderies.
La finesse et l'éclat de ces tapisseries.[2]

Not even Molière's miser, Harpagon, could avoid worrying over the horse carriage and the *porte cochère*. Nor was it unknown for people to feign a desirable antiquity of pedigree. According to one story, Colbert had the epitaph on his grandfather's tomb removed and replaced by one copied from the grave of a celebrated gentleman. Apocryphal or not, this anecdote is symbolic of the attempt of certain middle-class elements to pass from the bourgeoisie to the economic and social, if not hereditary, aristocracy.[3]

All such matters of conduct, aspiration, and style, however, were contained in a statutory system, which, in 1789 and for generations before, had divided France into three legal and political groups: the nobility, the clergy (the hierarchy of the Church), and the Third Estate. The last of these included all untitled Frenchmen, regularly domiciled and listed on the tax rolls, so that as part of the Third Estate, the bourgeoisie had no legal status of its own. Its social, professional, and economic place, on the other hand, was clear enough. The bourgeoisie stopped short of the "nobility of the robe" (members of the bureaucracy given titles for administrative and political services)* and it excluded "the people" (the manual workers). It embraced the intermediate ranks: financiers, industrialists, merchants, shopkeepers, revenue collectors, members of the universities and the professions, the intellectuals, and the lower clergy.[4]

Social historians are in the habit of speaking of the French Revolution as a revolution of the middle class. Before accepting this description, however, one must make certain distinctions between political agitation and social change. Marx, for exam-

* Because of their tradition of military service in the Middle Ages the members of the landed aristocracy were known as the "nobility of the sword."

ple, says that the protagonists of the French Revolution released clouds of rhetoric in the Roman senatorial style and called on the ghost of the Roman Republic in the process of assuming political power (just as he says that the English middle classes used Old Testament prose as moral propaganda to hide their attack on the aristocracy). And he suggests that such oratory was part of the natural ideological repertory of shopkeepers, importers, and stockholders, serving to ornament and give ethical blessing to their socioeconomic interests. But it is a matter of fact that not all of the bourgeoisie possessed such intellectual skills; nor was it, as a whole, inevitably pushed by circumstances to subvert French institutions in order to attain its aims. Many of the economic demands of the middle class were already a reality or likely to become one at the time of the convocation of the Estates-General by Louis XVI, and it is not only to the social origin but to the intellectual history of the delegates of the Third Estate that one must attribute their taste and gift for revolutionary politics. In the France of 1789, there was individual ownership of property, stocks, and bonds (as well as land); a protective tariff; patents and copyrights to protect inventors and writers; and much freedom of competition in trade and industry. However, the middle-class delegations to the Estates-General were almost all made up, not of shopkeepers and mill owners, but of functionaries and philosophical lawyers saturated with Voltaire and Montesquieu, the "law of nature," and "constitutional rights"—the product of a generation of literary coteries, smoking clubs, and *sociétés de pensée*. Marx might have added that, when the Estates-General became a national constitutional assembly, the best organizers and most effective politicians were either the most radical and impatient political theorists or men who worked with them. The abolition of feudal rights during the famous all-night session of August 4th, 1791, began with speeches calling for the legal or voluntary liquidation of feudalism made by the Viscount of Noailles and the Duke of Auillon, two of the several noblemen who had "gone over" to the bourgeoisie.[5]

Still, if the bourgeoisie as a class did not set out to cause a great historical overturn, it was certainly the beneficiary of it. In 1815, after Jacobinism, Thermidorianism, Bonapartism, and even the Bourbon restoration, nothing was left in France of the *noblesse de la robe,* the *noblesse de l'epée,* of provosts, manors guilds, baronial or ecclesiastical courts, feudal titles, or church lands. Nor could the returned kings who followed Napoléon in the seat of power restrain the bourgeoisie in its surge for complete political domination or the "pursuit, the struggle and the employment of money." [6] The second of them, Charles X, tried to, but he only provoked the end of his reign and the final exit of the House of Bourbon from French history.

If the Revolution of 1789 put an end to ancient French society and its institutions, the revolution which dethroned Charles X in 1830 consolidated, as a matter of law and of public hierarchy, the social processes to which 1789 had given such stimulus and point. In one word, it enthroned, constitutionally and economically, the bourgeoisie. There were in France, in 1830, the beginnings of political radicalism and of a working-class movement. But historians of quite different ideological professions agree that the immediate political arguments leading to the revolution—the attempt by Charles X to curtail electoral privileges, constitutional guarantees and freedom of the press—were a matter of concern to such bourgeois factions as the liberal monarchists and the conservative republicans. It is true that bourgeois workers and intellectual agitators were brought together in the streets of Paris during the barricade days of the 1830 revolution (the three "glorious days" of July 27, 28, and 29) and that, at this early moment, the question of who was ultimately to grasp the power may have hung in the balance. But there is no question that, in the end, it was the bourgeoisie who nursed events toward a political upheaval and smoothly

and confidently appropriated its results. François Guizot, who
was to become prime minister of the new regime and who was
one of those responsible for the eventual outcome of the revolt,
remembers what he calls "the tide of anarchy," which ran rampant through the working classes of Paris. Crowds of laboring
people surrounded him in the streets and followed him into the
houses of friends, asking for a constitution "in the name of the
people" and promising their support in return. But Guizot
never doubted that his role, as one of the middle class, was to
be revolutionary "without promoting a revolution." [7] Not every
businessman was as epigrammatic as Guizot (who in addition
to being a politician was a history professor), but many of
them seem to have acted spontaneously and quite ingeniously
on his principle. Workers from the printing shops of Paris were
among the first to reach the streets on the morning of the first
day of the revolution. (July 27), as indeed they had been directed to do by their employers the previous day. In Lyons,
when the news of what was happening in Paris arrived, the
merchants sent word to their employees to stop work and join the
movement or else be fired and denied future work. And in
Nantes one textile manufacturer was so proud of the part played
by his men at his prompting that he demanded to be given the
Cross of the Legion of Honor. Louis Blanc, whose accounts of
the period were written in a somewhat muckraking libertarian
spirit, said that the middle class swindled the workers out of a
revolutionary victory. But, even assuming that the workers were
fully ready, intellectually and politically, for a revolution of
their own (which Blanc does not show), it is difficult to see why
this is not another way of describing the dexterity of the bourgeoisie in securing the benefits of a revolt which they had led
and organized.[8]

In choosing a ruler in 1830, the bourgeoisie acted with almost instinctive sureness. Their choice, Louis Philippe of Orléans, was cousin to the unseated Charles X and carried with

him the aura of an ancient house and of the steadfastness of the
monarchic principle. But he could also claim for his political
ancestry a comfortable spirit of enlightenment and a friendly
outlook toward the new political day. His father, prototype of
the emancipated aristocrat and an ardent camp follower of the
intellectual agitation which preceded the revolution of 1789,
had sponsored every daring idea, from English-style politics
(and English-style clothes) to rationalist philosophy and aero-
static balloons. It was in his private gardens that some of the
crowds had gathered for the attack on the Bastille, and when,
after an absence, he returned to France after the jailing of
Louis XVI, he renounced all titles of nobility and was granted
the personal ideological gift of a new name, Philippe Egalité, by
the city of Paris. His son had himself been a member of political
clubs at the age of seventeen and an officer in the armies of revolutionary France against its royalist enemies. He would later escape for his life when the Jacobins took power. His father
was not so lucky. He was sent to the guillotine by the politicians
of the Terror, notwithstanding the fact that, as a member of the
Convention, he had voted the same sentence for cousin and
godfather, the king.

Looking on such a family past, Louis Philippe could stand
before the French people as a reassuringly liberal monarchist,
a patriot, a victim of political extremes, and a friend of moder-
ation; it was natural that the bourgeois should have turned to
him as one who embodied their political needs and their concept of the legitimate order. More than that, they saw in him the
incarnation of a personal ideal. Writing in *Le National* in 1830,
Louis Thiers—obviously thinking of Napoléon—had said that
France had had enough of glory and genius and was in need of
a ruler of "simple virtues, modest and solid." This was a wish
faithfully incarnated in Louis Philippe. Officialdom was to replace the aristocracy, and even the glamor of the crown was to
be brought to terms with the mundane propriety of the middle

class. He led a life of virtuous and thrifty domesticity (the queen, a prudent housewife, had her dresses made over to avoid excess expenditures). He was a graduate of the *École polytechnique* and knew what it was to earn a living, having served as a mathematics instructor in Switzerland while in exile. His predecessor on the throne was fond of plumed bonnets and had had himself anointed at a revival of the medieval coronation. Louis Philippe wore a plain hat, carried an umbrella, walked on foot through the mud, and bowed with democratic affability to his subjects in the streets. Châteaubriand murmured that the idolatry of a name had been abolished and that monarchy was no longer a religion. Louis Philippe was the citizen king, *le roi bourgeois*.[9]

Middle-class rule meant business encouragement and an expanding market. Iron production, coal consumption, and iron ore extraction more than doubled, and there was a huge increase in certain forms of industrialized agriculture. True factory conditions may have been lacking, particularly when compared with England, but it did not seem so to contemporary observers who wrote of the ascendance of the machine, the destruction of the small shop, and the recruitment of the industrial labor of hundreds and thousands into new "barracks" and "monasteries."[10] Commercial enterprise was the spirit which permeated the Orleanist regime in every aspect. Its first prime minister was a financier and so was its second, Casimir Perier, a founder of the Bank of France, owner of mines, textile factories, sugar refineries, distilleries, and foundries. Speculation and company promotion boomed. The king himself was a careful investor of the family income, especially in English stocks and bonds. Joint-stock companies and public utilities ventures, indulgently looked after by political favor, introduced an era of financial scandals famous in French history. Toward its end, de Tocqueville wrote, the monarchy of July assumed the ways of a trading company which conducted its every transaction with a view to the profit of its shareholders.[11]

In *La Coalition,** a play which opened two months after the July revolution, a locksmith and his mother engage in the following conversation:

Martel, the locksmith:

> I shall not lay down my hammer until the revolution has been completed.

Mother Martel:

> Is that so? Is the revolution not completed? Is not the king on his throne? Are not the merchants in their shops? The clerks in their offices? The troops in their barracks? Why are not the workers in their shops? [12]

Whether this exchange was intended for the edification of the working class or the reassurance of the propertied, it relied on the words of someone speaking with the authority of parenthood and the instinct for security of old age to ply acceptance of the new order. And this order was, according to Louis Philippe, a matter of economic stakes. Unlimited democracy, he said candidly, left property undefended while inciting enmity toward wealth. Therefore, it created fear for wealth and undermined that accumulative industriousness which was its source.[13] There were others, however, who looked upon property relations as the foundation of civic structure and for whom the mission of the bourgeoisie was to bring about a new canon of social morality. Of these the most self-persuaded and the most distinguished was François Guizot, a durable politician who served as member of parliament and minister of education, and as prime minister from 1840 to 1848. He was also a historian and an unapologetic bourgeois intellectual at a time when pained abhorrence of the bourgeoisie was the official emotion of most writers and artists, whether political or nonpolitical, radical or neo-feudal. In all aspects of his thinking, Guizot was dedicated to the transparent guardianship of class interests.

* This word, like the English *Combination,* was a name for workers' organizations.

His own father had gone to the guillotine during the Revolution, but he was himself able to look beyond that event to the Revolution's historical significance and to write that it had elevated his class to a point from which he would never consent to sink. He admired family relations among the bourgeois, their intimacy and the care of the parents for the children, and he understood that they had this character because never before had the first been so completely engaged in the instruction and social prospects of the second. And when he advised bourgeois parents to promote an academic education among their sons, he wanted to impress on them that the revolutionary power of modern ideologies could only be contained by intellectual dedication to the proper social order. Guizot's partisanship was sustained by a system of large convictions. For him the bourgeoisie was, by virtue of the patent reasonableness of its aims, the only class capable of bracing and steadying a society suffering, he said, from "moral dispersion" after generations of ideological cure-alls and doctrinaire overstimulation. The key to this needed reassembly of social forces was for him a new definition of the principle of sovereignty. Guizot divided human rights into legal and moral—justice, property, and security—which belonged to all men, and political, which belonged only to men capable of certain social virtues. He saw these as the virtues of productivity, of which the middle class was, as always, the great exemplar. But he was willing to recognize them in anyone who showed a desire to improve himself through the acquisition and increase of property, thereby becoming middle-class. Political rights, then, were not possessed but earned. The net political value of a man, was to be measured by those things which reflected his dedication to useful tasks, as they were understood by the leading economic groups, just as these groups, having the largest and most literal stake in society, could be expected to be most responsive to its well-being. Alexis de Tocqueville, who also wrestled with the problem of authority in modern society, felt that property as such could never be the foundation of a moral order. Guizot thought the opposite. For him morality was a question of diligence, just as poverty was the repayment of indolence or the outcome of incapacity. Property was not only the source of moral virtue but its index. Consequently, it was the source of social rights as well.[14]

It should be added that in the France of Louis Philippe these were not mere teachings or exhortations but the facts of law. Popular suffrage in France before the revolution of 1848 had actually reached its peak immediately after 1789, when something less than half a million had been given the vote. By introducing tax qualifications, the Bourbon restoration had brought this figure down to 100,000, chiefly landowners and wealthy merchants and manufacturers. The Orléans monarchy reduced the electoral tax to accommodate the middle businessman and certain professional groups, but no one beyond that. In 1846, out of a population of 35,000,000, the "legal nation," the electorate of France (and embodiment of Guizot's rights by merit) was 250,000.* [15] De Tocqueville wrote that, in 1830, the triumph of the middle class had been so vast that every political prerogative and, in fact, "the whole government, was confined

* According to Sherman Kent's study of Orleanist electoral law, no less than 82 per cent of the electorate was from the "landed bourgeoisie," with the remaining 18 per cent belonging to the entrepreneurial, commercial, and professional groups. *Electoral Procedure under Louis Philippe* (New Haven: Yale University Press, 1937), pp. 26 ff. But even if Kent is right, one has to take into consideration the political sway and the social impetus of the different bourgeois groups. If the landowner group had the greater share of the vote, the industrial and commercial bourgeoisie represented the more energetic elements in the economy. And one must recall the traditional rapport between dominant economic forces and the state in France. Business interests were obviously close to the monarchy, just as the king was obviously sensitive to their needs. From an intellectual point of view, as we shall see, Kent's distinction between a rural and an urban middle class was not important. Both were regarded by writers as guilty of the same stolid narrowmindedness which they called "bourgeois."

and, as it were, heaped up within the narrow limits of one class, to the statutory exclusion of all beneath and the actual exclusion of all above." [16]

NOTES TO CHAPTER I

1. Charles Morazé, *Les Bourgeois conquerants* (Paris: Librarie Armand Colin, 1957), especially pp. 120-129; Charles Morazé, *La Bourgeoisie française* (Paris: Librarie Armand Colin, 1947), p. 65; Edmond Coblot, *La Barrière et le niveau* (Paris: Félix Alcan, 1925); Joseph Aynard, *La Bourgeoisie française* (Paris: Librarie Perrin, 1934), pp. 289-340, Henri Sée, *La France economique et sociale au XVIII siècle* (Paris: Librarie Armand Colin, 1933), p. 4.

2. Cited in Aynard, *op. cit.,* p. 288.

3. Erich Auerbach, *Scenes from the Drama of European Literature* (New York: Meridian Books, 1959), p. 133; Aynard, *op. cit.,* p. 301. For the history of ethical values in the English middle class before the English revolution see Louis B. Wright, *Middle Class Culture in Elizabethan England* (Chapel Hill: The University of North Carolina Press, 1935).

4. George Izard, *Les Classes moyennes* (Paris: Editions Rieder, 1938), p. 5; Elinor Barber, *The Bourgeoisie in Eighteenth Century France* (Princeton: The University Press, 1955), Chapter II; Joseph Aynard, *op. cit.,* Chapter VIII; George Lefebvre, *The Coming of the Revolution* (New York: Vintage Books, 1958), pp. 33-49; Henri Sée, *op. cit.,* chapters III, IV, V.

5. Crane Brinton, *A Decade of Revolution, 1789-1799* (New York & London: Harper & Brothers, 1934), chapters I & II; Regina Pernoud, *Les Origines de la bourgeoisie française* (Paris: Presse Universitaire, 1947), pp. 90-91; Morazé, *Les Bourgeois conquerants,* p. 124; E. L. Woodward, *French Revolutions* (London: Oxford University Press, 1953), pp. 2 f.

6. Georg Brandes, *Main Currents in Nineteenth Century Literature* (6 vols.; London: William Heineman, 1923), V ("The Romantic School in France"), 1-2.

7. François Guizot, *Memoirs: The History of My Own Time* (4 vols.; London: Richard Bentley, 1858), II, pp. 2, 27.

8. Eugène Fournière, *Le Règne de Louis Philippe* (Paris: Jules Rouff et Cie., 1906); Octave Festy, *Le Mouvement ouvrier au debut de la monarchie de juillet* (Paris: Edouard Canely, 1908); E. Levasseur, *His-*

toire des classes ouvrières en France (Paris: Hachette et Cie., 1867), especially pp. 28-30; Louis Blanc, *The History of Ten Years, 1830-1840, or France under Louis Philippe* (2 vols.; Philadelphia: Lea and Blanchard, 1848), **I**, 87-203. John Plamenatz, *The Revolutionary Movement in France, 1815-71* (London-New York-Toronto: Longmans, Green and Co., 1952), Chapter III; J. P. T. Bury, *France, 1814-1940* (London: Methuen and Co., 1949), Chapter V.

9. John M. Allison, *Thiers and the French Monarchy* (Boston: Houghton Mifflin and Co., 1926), p. 97; J. Lucas Dubreton, *The Restoration and the July Monarchy* (New York: G. P. Putnam's Sons, 1929), pp. 117, 170.

10. For the view that French industrialization in the first half of the nineteenth century was not significant see J. H. Clapham, *The Economic Development of France and Germany* (Cambridge: University Press, 1951), pp. 53-68. For the opposite view see Henri Sée, *Histoire economique de la France: Les Temps modernes* (Paris: Félix Alcan, 1927); Louis Blanc, *op. cit.,* **I**, 536-537.

11. Charlotte Touzalin Muret, *French Royalist Doctrines since the Revolution* (New York: Columbia University Press, 1933), p. 88.

12. Cited in Festy, *op. cit.,* p. 70.

13. Walter Phelps Hall & William Stearn Davis, *The Course of Europe since Waterloo* (New York: D. Appleton Century, 1941), p. 45; Carlton Hayes, *A Political and Cultural History of Modern Europe* (2 vols.; New York: Macmillan Co., 1896), **I**, 6; Alexis de Tocqueville, *Recollections* (New York: Macmillan Co., 1896), p. 5.

14. Guizot, *op. cit.,* **I**, 28, 61-62, 227, **III**, 12, 25, 139. See also Muret, *op. cit.,* pp. 89-90; E. L. Woodward, *Three Studies in European Conservatism* (London: Constable and Co., 1929), pp. 129, 212; J. P. Mayer, *Political Thought in France from the Revolution to the Fourth Republic* (London: Routledge & Kegan Paul Ltd., 1943), p. 13.

15. Dubreton, *op. cit.,* pp. 54, 176; Sherman Kent, *Electoral Procedure under Louis Philippe* (New Haven: Yale University Press, 1937), pp. 26f.

16. De Tocqueville, *Recollections,* p. 6.

CHAPTER II

THE CLIMATE OF
INTELLECTUAL DISAFFECTION

WHATEVER THE ETHICS of Orleanist France it would be hard to
deny that they existed in an increasingly prosperous country.
Opportunism, political deals, outright swindles, legitimate business, and industrial pioneering were all part of the economics of
this period. Yet this curious scramble (examples of which may
be discovered in the history of other nations in the early stages
of economic modernization) fostered, in the end, an enlarged
measure of material well-being. There was greater production,
greater consumption, wider trade, and higher technology. There
was exploitation, but, on the whole, the savings of the workers
increased. Even Stendhal, who directed a lifetime of dedicated
scorn at the spirit of the bourgeois monarchy, was reluctantly
forced to recognize this. There were, he said, so many new
buildings, farm improvements, and roads that he could not write
of them for fear of being taken as a government hack.[1]

When this is considered, the most important question for the
cultural historian of the period is to determine why its climate of

economic bluster was met by a mood of intellectual withdrawal and distrust. This was an energetic age whose leaders, according to Mrs. Trollope, the celebrated chronicler of nineteenth-century manners, were "a new race of Frenchmen." She meant, of course, the Orleanist businessman who accumulated capital "merrily" and with "almost American rapidity," and "every line of whose jocund face . . . and portly figure spoke contentment and well-being." [2] It was also an age whose literary heroes were afflicted young men gazing with bitter wisdom on a betraying world or outcasts from workaday society caring only for beauty or adventure. For businessmen the times beamed with opportunities to be harvested by ingenuity and ambition. Literary spirits, looking at the same landscape, saw nothing but the desolation left behind by a tide of cupidity and triviality. What we must remember, however, is that most of the writers and artists were also children of the middle class,* and this raises an obvious sociological riddle: how did it happen that while one section of the bourgeoisie was efficiently gathering profits with unbending matter-of-factness, another was giving itself over to philosophical despair, the cult of sensitivity, and the enthronment of the nonutilitarian virtues?

As frequently happens, the dominant forces of a society will embrace or prod the people of that society with a seemingly undivided sweep of purpose, while dissenting influences struggle along many turns and fall into many moods. And so it was with literary discontent. For instance, Petrus Borel, a poet who liked to call himself a lycanthrope or werewolf, paraded himself as a republican at a time when republicanism was suspect or even subversive. This behavior might appear, at first, as the gesture of man with a courageous concern for social questions. But this would be a pointedly equivocal inference, since what Borel conceived as republicanism was precisely the opposite, a kind of

---

* With the exception of Pierre Proudhon (who came from an artisan, not a proletarian, family) it would be difficult to think of a significant nineteenth-century French intellectual of working-class origin.

legalization of social disarray which would afford the most in-
dulgent opportunities for his personal imagination and taste. He
was a "republican," he said, because he could not be a savage
Indian. And should the promises of political disorder fail to
materialize in France, he was ready to sail for America and the
wild remoteness of Missouri to which he would carry his last,
ailing illusion.[3] At other times this kind of extravagant and care-
free egotism would succumb to an unconquerable sense of futility which rendered the individual powerless to envision social
purpose or made that purpose seem empty even when attaina-
ble. Thus in *Obermann,* his apology for suicide, Étienne de
Senancour complained, not of the burden of misfortune, but of
the fatigue of tedium and of the already lost battle against
monotony and triviality.[4]

The literary mind of the Orleanist period was caught in a battle between intellectual ardor and intellectual helplessness; it
was tormented by a sense of trepidation, indecisiveness, and
ultimate fear, even in the midst of momentary excitement
created by the adventure of a new social epoch.

Our period was a mixture of activity, hesitation and idleness; of bril-
liant Utopias, philosophic or religious aspirations, vague enthusiasms . . . boredom, discord, and uncertain hopes. Ambition was
not of our age . . . and the greedy race for position and honors
drove us away from spheres of political activity. There remained to
us only the poet's ivory tower where we mounted ever higher to
isolate ourselves from the crowd. In those high altitudes we breathed
at last the pure air of solitude; we drank forgetfulness in the golden
cup of legend; we were drunk with poetry and love.[5]

This was written by the poet Gérard de Nerval—and unmistakable cry of defensive idealism, frail, rhapsodic, and, in its devotion to a private perfection, a moment of homage to sentiments of noble impotence. Perhaps de Nerval knew this when
he wrote it, for he killed himself in mid-life in 1855.

Ennui, said Alfred de Musset, was the ailment of the age.
George Sand, one of whose novels was dedicated to the new

sensibility, explained it as the curse of a uniquely self-conscious generation victimized by its own painful brilliance and visionary strain which had produced "monstrous sufferings" unknown to psychology until then.[6] This is not surprising since Sand herself was a spirit in upheaval. But for an orthodox Catholic writer like the young Lamennais* these battling inner afflictions were not causes but symptoms. Intellectual rebelliousness and grief, he said, became suicidal sentiment because they were essentially egotistical and their causes were not very different from those of actual suicide as a social phenomenon. When men were held within "the empire of religious ideas" suicide had been rare, but now it was common because a "sore" had been opened in men's minds by the secularism and skepticism of the eighteenth century and by the Revolution, a sore which no aesthetic illusion or pure intellectual passion could cure. Man, by his new faithlessness, had triumphed in the task of making himself a degraded king ruling over his own misery.[7]

By the "empire of religious ideas" Lamennais meant not only the realm of personal conviction, but a bond of human and social recognition which had its expression, as well as its cement, in a community of spiritual principles. It was really a way of saying that suicide, like intellectual willfulness (and despair), was the equivocal gift of a public order which was no longer echoed in the intimate lives of sensitive men. Other writers saw this too, though as a cultural, not a religious impasse. Speaking of the restiveness of his generation, de Nerval said that it was not unlike other crises "which ordinarily follow great revolutions or the decline of great reigns." Aphoristically, though perhaps not too originally, de Musset spoke of the twin injuries of the heart; all that had been was no longer, and all that would be was not yet.[8]

It is quite evident that in all these words one finds not only the voicing of a problem, but an active wish for desolation and

---

* A defender of Catholic tradition in his early years, Lamennais ended his life as a rebel against the Church.

inner injury. This does not discount their meaning. On the contrary, it is just such a will to unhappiness and such a search for heartaches that marks them as a cultural expression. The homelessness and agitation of men stranded in the midst of confusion was real enough. However, it was not just something largely and inexpressively "historical." It was also the product of specific events which had affected the conditions of intellectual life since the end of the eighteenth century. An altered order of society had changed the nature of the literary market and the literary trade. It had created and demanded a new view of the relations between the public and the man of letters and a new definition of the source and the function of literary work.

The imagination of the nineteenth century liked to look on the literary act as something rising before the eyes of society from out of the individual alone, because its origins were mysteriously webbed within him. It will be our task to understand how something so privately conceived was actually part of a language with which the creative person sought to control, to reject, or even to exorcise the onset of new historical realities.

NOTES TO CHAPTER II

1. Sée, *Histoire économique,* p. 226.

2. Frances Trollope, *Paris and the Parisians in 1835* (New York: Harper & Bros., 1836), pp. 74, 91-92.

3. S. A. Rhodes, *Gérard de Nerval* (New York: Philosophical Library, 1951), pp. 42-43.

4. Étienne de Senancour, *Obermann* (Paris: Eugene Pasquelle, 1901).

5. Cited in Rhodes, *op. cit.,* pp. 54-55.

6. De Senancour, *op. cit.,* pp. 154-165.

7. F. de Lamennais, *Oeuvres complètes* (Bruxelles: Hauman et Cie., 1839), I, 151.

8. Alfred de Musset, *La Confession d'un enfant du siècle* (Paris: Charpentier, 1862), p. 22.

CHAPTER III

THE EMPIRE OF PARIS
AND THE
INTELLECTUAL OUTCAST

IN FRANCE," said Montesquieu, "there is only Paris and a few provinces that Paris hasn't yet found time to gobble up." [1] Montesquieu may have written these words less as a historical observer than as a cosmopolitan sage looking forward to the eventual subjection of unworldly provincialism. He was, all the same, speaking of a historical movement toward the domination of French cultural and political life by the capital, never broken since the beginnings of French national life and only accelerated and perfected by the events of the Revolution. Like all great cities, Paris was a center of elegance, art, learning, poverty, and crime. It had a vast scholarly population (about 11,000 university and professional students) and, according to municipal lists, an even larger indigent population. It had an equal number of establishments for the dispensation of charity and the creation of *haute couture* and restaurants, of which Thackeray said that nothing could be more exquisite or beautiful. It had great museums; botanical gardens; historical monuments;

writers' and scientists' salons; coffee houses, which cradled celebrated literary coteries; twenty-seven theaters (London, with
twice the population, had only eighteen);* as well as street shows
featuring Moroccan dancing girls, Siamese twins, mechanical
men, and other gifts to the popular thirst for wonders and cheap
exoticism.[2] Surrounding it all was the big-city spectacle of
roguery and picturesque marginality: confidence men, petty
racketeers, "characters," dandies, sports, peddlers of pseudo-
scientific frauds, and many other enterprising exploiters of car-
nality, innocence, and greed, who according to Thackeray, could
be found in Paris "in greater number than in any other European
nursery." [3]

Mrs. Trollope says that it was a certain effervescence of animal spirits that gave Paris its indescribable air of gaiety and
made it a "city of the living" above all others. Though no doubt
true, this statement is one of sentiment, not of explanation.
However, another of Mrs. Trollope's observations brings the life
of the city closer to the grasp of the social historian. Its rousing
charm, she felt, was in part created by the "busy idleness" of a
place where so many people had "nothing to do but to divert
themselves and others." [4] John Scott, one of Mrs. Trollope's
traveling predecessors found Paris as pleasurably arresting as she
had. He called it a "glass beehive," a "treat to the student of
humanity," the essence of whose existence was "the consciousness of being observed" and gave a similar explanation, the
presence, striking for an Englishman, he said, of people who
seemed "loose from any actual occupation." [5] The point of both
comments was the same. In dominating the life of the provinces
and becoming the main agency and clearinghouse for every sort
of interest from politics to business, luxury, entertainment, and
pleasure, Paris was bound to attract all those who had come to
the city to make a living from its many incidental activities: the
floater, the sharp, the playboy, and the shadowy entrepreneur—

* The population of Paris went from 774,338 in 1831 to 935,261 in
1842 and 1,053,000 in 1846.

people whose existence was essentially improvised, unconventional, ingeniously opportunistic, full of an easygoing lust for fun, and who, for that reason, became actors in the pageant of self-amusement which Mrs. Trollope found so pleasant.

Roaming marginals were not, as such, a new thing. Already at the close of the Old Regime, Sébastien Mercier had found the young men of Paris irreverent, heartless, "impudent, bold of eye . . . eternally moving, eternally idle, a prey to all vices; seeking in vain to hide under affected arrogance of demeanor their entire unimportance to the world." [6] If nothing else, this shows that the emergence of an anchorless and rebellious new generation in the midst of urban society is not a creation of our day. It also anticipates the nineteenth-century literary revolt, so much of which was filled with the deification of outcast youth and the bitter disavowal of the old. But more important for the moment is to recognize the appearance of the foot-loose intellectual as one of the figures in the world of "those who get by," the *viveurs* of the city. This was a fact noted both by social observers and incidental popular writers. In *Lost Illusions,* Balzac described the *viveurs* as "some rich, others poor, all equally idle . . . who, with no outlet for their energies, threw themselves not only into journalism and conspiracies, literature and art, but into the most extravagant excesses and dissipations." [7] Henri de Mürger's account of the *vie de bohème,* a best-selling success, the source of a well-known opera, and the model for many other chronicles of the life of the garret, begins with an admonition to the reader not to confuse the book's geniuses with the key-ring peddlers and confidence men of the boulevards.[8]

It is true that the chief explanation given by Balzac for the dissipated ardor of the young *viveurs* was the frustrating political conditions of the restoration period which, he said, had wasted their energies and enslaved them in inactivity. Yet, there were many reasons, atmospheric, occupational, and institutional, why the aspiring and dispossessed intellectuals should mass their numbers in Paris. The traditional volatility and ex-

citement of the city were, of course, there; "idea-distribution is
the function of Paris," said Victor Hugo.[9] In *Les Français peints
par eux-mêmes*—a good-humored but admiring catalogue of the
city's cultural opulence—we read that the mere mention of its
name was sufficient to make tears roll from the eyes of provincial literati. Paris was not only the arbiter and dictator of the
theater, the arts and the publishing business, it was also the
only major educational market open to French youth.[10] A
Napoleonic ordinance of 1815 had commanded the simultane-
ous creation of fifteen departmental universities. But the plan
had failed through its own ambitiousness; and when, in 1836,
the Chamber of Deputies looked around the country for an
educational system which would meet the needs of a "numerous
and spirited youth demanding a career and solid studies," it
could find none.[11] The same complaints were made by the philosopher Victor Cousin in 1840 and, in 1842, by François
Guizot, then minister of education. Paris, according to Guizot,
"stuffed itself" with promising minds, robbing the rest of France
of places where the provincial youth could be trained for a useful and "honorable career." [12]

This problem was made all the more acute by the narrow
French conception of "honorable career," a term which meant,
above all, the traditional professions of medicine, the academy,
and the law; that is to say, the very callings which, by the very
exclusiveness of their respectability, tended to become over-
crowded. There were other acceptable occupations, of course:
business, engineering, the government, politics. But each of
these had certain handicaps. Under the Orleanist system elective
positions were unsalaried, and this meant that political careers
often entailed heavy financial burdens. As for the new technological professions, the demand for them was not yet widespread. And finally, because of the tremendous pull of Paris,
there were always many people waiting to get into the state
bureaucracy. In 1831, according to one source, the city had
40,000 office-seekers.[13]

Paris not only attracted its literary *declassées* but manufactured them, and some contemporary accounts are realistic and off-hand enough to attribute the super-abundance of intellectual fervor to nothing more lofty than occupational frustration. Scarcely a few of the thousands of young provincials who came to Paris every year, says *Les Français peints par eux-mêmes,* arrived at the stage-coach depot with the formal intention of becoming men of letters. Most expected to study law or medicine, and it was only after failing in this that their minds began to be filled with poetry and high thought.[14] Literary periodicals, Alexandre Dumas *père* explained, had their genesis when a literary man without books met a doctor without patients and a lawyer without clients over a dinner to be paid with their last pennies. What to do? The answer was simple; start a journal. Paper and printing could be had on credit. Gall and *esprit* they already had.[15] At the same time, the fact that letters could be conceived as a career without the elaborate training and initiation which other professions required was made possible by the convenient broadness, both topical and technical, which the literary trade had come to develop under the social dispensation of the post-revolutionary period. An aristocracy, says Alexis de Tocqueville, looks upon society as a finished and permanently contrived reality whose ideas are attached to a scale of unchanging models and whose literature written under such sponsorship rests on concepts of craft guided by acknowledged canons of content and style.[16] But the end of the traditional society not only changed the public character of the writer. It initiated a debate concerning the claims and duties of readers toward him and his own obligations and powers. It destroyed the customary sense of literary discipline and the character of literary art.

What was the center of the new literary order, the modern man of letters? Louis Culmer, the editor of *Les Français peints par eux mêmes,* who wanted his long (eight volumes) work to be a spiritual encyclopaedia of nineteenth-century French life, commissioned the essayist Élias Regnault to answer this very question. But Regnault declared himself helpless before such an equivocal subject and told the editor to try it himself. Entering this contest in farcical despair, Culmer at once proclaimed his own paralysis, and when Regnault eventually wrote the piece he could produce nothing more than a record of ambiguities. Grocers and pharmacists had their stock in trade, he explained, but modern writers had no longer an ordained skill nor a sure professional manner. Instead one found numberless postulants to a mutable title contested in assorted fashions. Musicians were presumed to read music and carpenters to handle a plane, but men of letters simply announced themselves. "It is a title," wrote Regnault, suddenly shifting from satire to denunciation, "that serves to hide mediocrity and social uselessness." [17]

Regnault's troubles in defining the man of letters—if the species had existed at the time of Noah, he said, the Ark would not have been large enough to hold its many varieties—were in every way comparable to the inability of the editors of *Le Diable à Paris* (like Culmer's *Les Français,* a collection of essays on modern art life) to establish the nature of "a book." After their own round of irony the editors concluded that a modern book dealt with any subject matter qualifying as "matter," that is, having "height, length, and width sufficient to make a square stack of printed paper." A man of letters was, of course, the author of a "book." [18]

In other words, through the gathering of a large marginal population in a great city, the scarcity of "honorable" occupations, and the professional ambiguity of the new literature, that peculiar version of the self-made man, the roving intellectual, had become a permanent feature of Parisian life. According to Mrs. Trollope, a "swarm of tiny geniuses that settle in clusters" populated the newspapers, the theaters, and the fiction outlets.[19] One writer boasted that there were in Paris 6,000 young men willing to give their lives for the sake of art,[20] and *Le Diable à Paris* agreed that nowhere could one find so many literary toilers as in Paris.[21] Literature, said Dumas, had become the most characteristic and most epidemic folly of youth. There was no child who did not begin a classical tragedy in the fifth grade and finish it in the seventh, and even professionals and business-men remained secretly haunted by literary reveries of their school days.[22] Writing in the 1840's Louis Culmer said that any editor foolish enough to advertise an interest in manuscripts did so at his peril, for he would only be inviting the beginning work of adolescents, the effusions of society ladies, and the sparetime thoughts of provincial clerks and tax collectors.

Every day his mail disgorges manuscripts. It is a torrent, a cataclism. It is useless to try to flee the storm. . . . The door bell rings, it is a manuscript. He leaves the house, there's a manuscript on the front steps. He returns home avoiding the main entrance, there is a manu-script on the back steps.[23]

The editor had become the drowning casualty of cultural over-production.

NOTES TO CHAPTER III

1. Cited in Alexis de Tocqueville, *The Old Regime and the French Revolution* (New York: Doubleday Anchor Books, 1955), p. 74.

2. J. L. Belin and A. Pujol, *Histoire civile, morale, et monumentale de Paris* (Paris: Belin-Leprieur, 1943), pp. 560, 578; Henri d'Almeras, *La Vie parisienne sous le règne de Louis-Philippe* (Paris: Albin Michel, n.d.), pp. 1, 17; Jacques Antoine Dulaure, *Histoire de Paris* (Paris: Furne et Cie., 1846), p. 652 (figures for 1846); Walter Besant, *London in the Nineteenth Century* (London: Adam and Charles Black, 1909), pp. 11, 17; William Makepeace Thackeray, *The Paris Sketch Book* (London: Smith, Elder and Co., 1870), p. 229.

3. Thackeray, *op. cit.,* pp. 19, 259.

4. Trollope, *op. cit.,* pp. 108, 26, 39.

5. John Scott, *A Visit to Paris* (1815), p. 53.

6. Helen Simpson, ed., *The Waiting City* (London: G. G. Harrap and Co., 1933) (a translation and abridgement of Louis Sébastien Mercier's *Le Tableau de Paris,* 1782-1788), pp. 278-279.

7. Honoré de Balzac, *Lost Illusions* (London: John Lehman, 1951), pp. 422-423.

8. Henri Mürger, *Scenes de la vie de bohème* (Paris: Michel Levy Frères, 1874), p. 1.

9. Victor Hugo, *Paris* (Paris: Calman Levy, 1879).

10. *Les Français peints par eux-mêmes: Encyclopaedie morale du dix-neuvième siècle,* Louis Culmer, ed. (8 vols.; Paris: Schneider and Lagrand, 1941), **VIII,** 232. The essays in this collection are literary, not historical or sociological, and their information cannot be taken as absolutely factual. But they do describe Parisian life with a wealth of detail which, in the balance, must be regarded as significant.

11. Louis Liard, *L'Enseignement supérieur en France* (2 vols.; Paris: Armand Colin, 1894), **I,** 182-183.

12. *Ibid.,* p. 184.

13. Walter Phelps Hall & William Stearn Davis, *The Course of Europe since Waterloo* (New York: Appleton-Century, 1941), p. 86.

14. *Les Français,* **I,** 34.

15. Alexandre Dumas, *Souvenirs dramatiques* (2 vols.; Paris: Michel Levy Frères, 1868) **I,** p. 175.

16. De Tocqueville, *Democracy in America,* **II,** 56 *et seq.*

17. *Les Français,* **III,** 223.

18. George Sand *et al., Le Diable à Paris* ("Paris et les Parisiens") (2 vols.; Paris: J. Hetzel, 1845). **I,** 121.

19. Trollope, *op. cit.,* p. 53.

20. Albert Joseph George, *The Development of Romanticism in France* (Syracuse: University Press, 1955), p. 79.

21. *Le Diable à Paris,* **I,** 21.

22. Dumas, *op. cit.,* p. 173.

23. *Les Français,* **III,** 222.

CHAPTER IV

THE NEW
LITERARY MARKET

ONE OF THE LOWLIEST among those struggling to make their way in the ungoverned, crowded arena of the new literature was a figure whom we will easily recognize as a stock character of contemporary culture, the perennially destitute writer surviving from day to day in a world of "little magazines" and rejection slips. We encounter him in *Les Français peints par eux-mêmes* as the "débutant littéraire," a young provincial sent to Paris by his father to study "procedural law and good manners" and who, after some time in the big city, renounces his career and finds himself both penniless and intellectually emancipated. In his explorations, the young man hears of the prices commanded by successful authors. He awakens the next day in a condition of "débutant littéraire," and soon the first of a number of articles is on the way. However, these articles never get beyond the tangle of quibbling loyalties and stiff particularisms which comprise modern taste. One journal judges them too immoral, another too puritanically passé. For some editors they are too conservative, for others too incendiary. For some they are too sentimental and banal, for others too eccentric and naughty.

The "débutant," about to be driven back to the law and, ultimately, to the province where he will practice it, happens on a poster advertising *The Cherub,* a literary journal which has never rejected his writings for the simple reason that he had never known of its existence. *The Cherub* has three principal characteristics. It is printed on pink paper, it has a youthful staff pledged to a literary revolution; and it is bankrupt. When the "débutant" arrives at *The Cherub*'s office (which also serves as sleeping quarters for contributors who are behind in their rent) he is told that, rather than new writers, the magazine needs new subscribers. He subscribes at once and the question then becomes: can *The Cherub* refuse to publish the work of one of its subscribers? It cannot, of course. At last the young provincial makes his debut —in *The Cherub*'s last issue.[1]

This burlesque and its subject, the "little magazine," are entirely familiar to us: the sacrifices and obscure self-dedication of the young editors, the *recherché* format, the faith in the power of ideas to infect the world, the esoteric momentousness of it all. There were, however, other more efficient and less lonely means of literary publicity. One was the salon and the other the *cénacle.* The salon was only a continuation of the informal gathering of the Old Regime which brought intellectuals together and allowed the hosts to witness the most fashionable literary battles of the day. According to some historians the salons of the seventeenth and eighteenth centuries had existed primarily to promote polite conversation between intellectuals and socialites, an art which Talleyrand had called "the most beautiful and greatest joy of man." [2] What the nineteenth-century salon provided was a semi-formal audience and a place where writers could meet publishers and find leads into those areas of intellectual life dependent on organized sponsorship, such as the opera and the state-supported theaters.[3] In an article entitled "How I became a dramatic author," Alexandre Dumas *père* relates how Charles Naudier, a literary critic and the leader of a successful salon, got him an interview with Baron Taylor, *Commissaire Royal* for the *Théâtre Français,* and how this interview suddenly and decisively opened for him the way to a literary career.[4]

The *cénacle* resembled the salon in some respects but might be "technically" distinguished from it in that it was an assembly of the intellectuals themselves. It could, for this reason, play a more confident and original role. In fact, when a *cénacle* fell under the spiritual emperorship of some great figure, its devotion of stylistic and doctrinal principles was aroused to something more than rhetoric. One example of this was the encounter between Victor Hugo's *cénacle* and the theater audience at the première of Hugo's play *Hernani* in 1830. It had been anticipated (correctly) that the novelties of the play would cause derision, surprise, and indignation, and straight-faced conspiratorial preparations were made to meet this challenge, including the identification of the conspirators by secretly exchanged pieces of paper containing the Spanish code word *hierro* (iron). When the day came, Hugo's partisans appeared at the theater defiantly costumed in a variety of Bohemian styles and armed with walking canes and either smothered the opposition with their cheers or actually clubbed it into silence. The "battle of Hernani" in time became *the* schoolbook anecdote marking the beginnings of romantic drama in France.

Far more decisive, as concrete social and economic factors affecting literary production, were the appearance of a large-scale reading public, the almost wholly commercial organization of cultural distribution (of art and music as well as literature), and the great increase in literary output. Some historians attribute the development of mass literacy to the educational work of the French Revolution. Others date true elementary education from a law of 1835.[5] All that can be said is that, judging from the number and circulation of newspapers and the fees paid writers who worked for them, a very sizable popular audience was already in existence at the time of Louis Philippe. In Paris alone, the number of dailies went from eleven in 1811 to thirteen in 1824 to twenty-six in 1846, and the total number of their subscribers from 56,000 to 200,000.[6] In the tradition founded by the French Revolution, which carried in a swelling flow into the nineteenth century, many of these publications were organs for doctrinal discussion and socio-philosophical advocacy. There were traditionalist, working-class, Saint-Simonian, feminist, and Catholic newspapers and magazines. There was *Le Conservateur, Le Réformateur,* and *L'Observateur.* There was *L'Avenir, Le Contemporain* and *La Revue Rétrospective, Le Légitimiste, Le Franc Royaliste, L'Idée Napoléonienne,* and *Le Républicain.*[7] Thirteen different journals of ideas were published in Paris, at one time or another, during the reign of Louis Philippe (twice as many as in all of the British Isles for the same period) and approximately 130 other publications advertised cultural discussion among their features, though perhaps this was done only as a prestige label to indicate the literate rather than the literary intentions of the publishers. On the other hand, there were several entertainment sheets which were in part literary and a number of humor magazines of the satirical literary type. It seems fairly clear that all of the big dailies gave prominent play to literary and art topics.[8] There was also a genuine popular press. France had been backward (if that is the word) in the creation of a commercialized press when one compares it with England which, since the eighteenth century, had known such forms of contemporary journalism as the gossip item, the specialized column and the "true story" narrative.[9] Nevertheless a reading of Eugène Hatin's massive *Bibliographie historique et critique de la presse périodique française* shows that a number of the familiar specimens—the woman's magazine, the digest review, the special interest sheet, and the humorous weekly—were already in circulation by 1830.[10]

As for the book trade, some of the figures given by historians for the number of books published during this period are so large that it is nearly impossible to believe them. But there is no question of the great upsurge in book printing. In fact, there is evidence that, at first, the new publishing industry did not know how to keep expansion from becoming a mere glut and that the sharp rise in the number of books published before 1826 actually represented a series of overproduction crises which eventually required Louis Philippe to come to the rescue with a grant of 10,000,000 francs.[11] The introduction of volume sales as a law of the intellectual trade was bound to affect both the writers, and the buyers and distributors of their services. The old book printer gave way to the modern publisher, a man who conceived of himself as a businessman and an investment gambler, able to sense popular demands and to gauge bestseller possibilities. For the commercial publisher the literary work was only the beginning. Like any other product, it had to be marketed in such a way as to insure a return on the investment. New style publishers (like the well-known L'Advocat) advertised their books with color posters, made themselves pleasant to the staff of important newspapers (without neglecting "prestige" publications), and hopefully and persistently presented critics with complimentary copies.[12] There was nothing poetic, Regnault said in *Les Français peints par eux-mêmes,* about the merchandising side of literature, either on the part of publishers or authors.

There are first class items in intelligence as in any other kind of commodity. They have their market price, like asphalt or Marseille soap. Spiritual rates shift in the same fashion as industrial rates.[13]

Speaking of newspapers, Lytton Bulwer wrote that at stockholder meetings shouting, spouting men sat about discussing the value of an opinion "as the value of rice, indigo or any marketable commodity." [14] The authors themselves, while unknown, appeared as self-effacing and patient men, gratefully dropping into their pockets whatever the publisher might choose to pay them for their long nights of work. But an upswing in their market value could turn them into dictators who argued over the price of each line, quarreled over its length and counted letters one by one. The man of letters, remarked Regnault, wished to be a cultural functionary presiding over the hierarchy of civilized values, while he dispensed his product in a way no different from the industrial worker, the grocer, or the fruit peddler.[15]

A chief source of the high prices paid to writers and, perhaps, the most profitable literary novelty of the nineteenth century, was the newspaper serialization of their novels. Alexandre Dumas *père* wrote 100,000 lines a year for *Le Siècle* at 1.50 francs a line.[16] Eugène Sue was paid 100,000 by *Le Constitutional* for *The Wandering Jew*. Lamartine got 250,000 from *La Presse* for the *History of the Girondins*.[17]* In turn serialized literature proved a tremendous circulation builder. When Eugène Sue joined *Le Constitutionnel* circulation jumped from 3,000 to 40,000. *Le Siècle* picked up 100,000 new readers after it started publishing *Le Capitain Paul* by Dumas *père* for which he was paid 100,000 francs.[18] An inevitable outgrowth of this was the use of publicity stunts and the fabrication of customer intrigue and anxiety as means of merchandising literature. At times the publication of a serial novel was interrupted without explanation in order to create the impression that the author was ill and, perhaps, unable to produce the next installment, when, in fact, the novel had been written and delivered in advance. "The puffing and advertising" used by the publishers of the serials, said one observer, "would make even an American stare." [19] "Industrialized literature," Sainte-Beuve called it, which happens to describe well the methods of its greatest practitioner, Alexandre Dumas, *père,* who kept a stable of ghost writers readying manuscripts for his signature. In one of the literary jokes of the period the elder Dumas asks his son, also a novelist, "Have you seen my latest work?" and Dumas *fils* answers, "No, father, have you?" Yet regard-

* *La Presse* was published by Émile de Girardin, who created the modern popular newspaper in France by introducing cheap subscription rates and high advertising income.

less of open or subtle deprecation, profits were important to the writer as a source of status in a money-conscious society. A story in *Les Français peints par eux-mêmes* describes a bourgeois who hears that the playwright Scribe gets 5,000 to 6,000 francs for a short piece. He goes home resolved to put an end to his son's pharmaceutical career and turn him into a man of letters.[20]

What is peculiar, when one turns from the economics of modern literature to the self-image and social emotions of the writers themselves is that, despite the amount of money spent for the purchase of literary production, the life of the writer was seen more than ever as a drama of cruel and erratic odds, leading in one direction to golden elegance and glory and in the other to despair. Actually such a response was the psychological companion to a cultural market which was in itself paradoxical. The means of reward—circulation and money—had been standardized and so had some forms of literature like the serial novel and the popular theater. Still, it was impossible for all writers to relate to the market in the same way because so much of the serious (or seriously intended) literature of the period was becoming increasingly personal and diversified and had nothing for the predictable public, which supported pulp stories, light comedy, and the melodrama. And there was no market large enough for the growing numbers of literary aspirants. Some forms of realism, like Balzac's, made fortunes. Others, like Stendhal's (in spite of Balzac's written praise) did not. Some of Stendhal's novels sold less than one hundred copies.[21] Dumas *père* received 300,000 for one play.[22] Serial novel fees allowed Eugène Sue to spend hours with his tailor discussing fine points of fashion. Baudelaire, a man of equal fastidiousness and surely greater talent, had to bargain unpleasantly with his mother for spending money. Literature, said Mürger, was the road to acclaim or to the morgue. This is an exaggerated statement in the characteristically agonized chiaroscuro of the romantic period. But it speaks in some sense for the dazzled hopes and qualms of the writer as he tried to take the measure of his place in a changed society.

NOTES TO CHAPTER IV

1. *Les Français,* **I**, 54-56.

2. Funck-Brentano, *La Vie parisienne a l'époque romantique* (Paris: Payot, 1931), pp. 27-28.

3. Henri Avernel, *Histoire de la presse française* (Paris: Ernest Flammarion, 1900), p. 366.

4. André le Breton, *Le Théâtre romantique* (Paris: Boivin et Cie., n. d.), pp. 18-19.

5. George Coignot, *La Question scolaire en 1848 et les lois falloux* (Paris: Edition Hier et Aujourd'hui, 1948), pp. 50-51; Albert Joseph George, *The Development of French Romanticism* (Syracuse: University Press, 1955).

6. Henry Lytton Bulwer, *The Monarchy of the Middle Classes* (2 vols.; London: Richard Bentley, 1836), **I**, 54; George, *op. cit.,* p. 61; Henri Avernel, *op. cit.,* p. 370.

7. Eugène Hatin, *Bibliographie historique et critique de la presse periodique française* (Paris: Firmin Bidot, 1866), passim.

8. *Ibid.,* passim.

9. Leo Lowenthal & Majorie Fisk, "The Debate over Art and Popular Culture in Eighteenth Century England." In *Common Frontiers in the Social Sciences,* Mirra Komarovsky, ed. (Glencoe, Ill.: The Free Press, 1959).

10. Hatin, *op. cit.,* pp. 367-435.

11. George, *op. cit.,* p. 44.

12. Jules Bertaut, *L'Époque romantique* (Paris: J. Tallandier, 1947), p. 112.

13. *Les Français,* **III**, 226.

14. Bulwer, *op. cit.,* **I**, 56.

15. *Les Français,* **III**, 229-232.

16. George, *op. cit.,* p. 45.

17. Bertaut, *op. cit.,* p. 24.

18. George, *op. cit.,* pp. 63-65.

19. Albert Dresden Vandam, *An Englishman in Paris* (2 vols.; London: Chapman & Hall, 1892), **I**, 56.

20. *Les Français,* **I**, 34-35.

21. Pompeyo Gener, *Literaturas malsanas* (Barcelona: Juan Llordachs, 1900), p. 190.

22. F. W. Draper, *The Rise and Fall of the French Romantic Drama* (London: Constable & Co., 1923), p. 164.

CHAPTER V

THE MODERN MAN
OF LETTERS AS
A SOCIAL PROBLEM

DURING THE OLD REGIME, as during the classical age of patronage in general, the position of the man of letters had often been that of a specialized retainer of the upper class. This, naturally enough, has caused historians to ask themselves whether such a system was not harrowing to the literary artist and damaging to his personal and creative integrity. Did Shakespeare mean it when, in the dedication of *The Rape of Lucrece* he said to his patron, "What I have done is yours," [1] or Poliziano when he wrote to Lorenzo de Medici, "I desire no other muse or other gods but you?" [2]

Although there is some evidence to show that writers did at times feel annoyed by the necessity of catering to sponsors, this question must, on the whole, be regarded as rhetorical. The aristocracy happened to be the accepted ambit within and for which, literature and art were largely created. They were the writer's chief dependable source of remuneration. This meant having to endure a certain etiquette of deference which, for

instance, allowed Lord Halifax to interrupt the formal reading
of Pope's translation of Homer to suggest improvements
(though, characteristically, the poet took this as an expected
occurrence and made no complaint).[3] Still, we must remember
that there could exist between artist and patron a cultural com-
mensalism which granted the artist the favors of the patron
while schooling the patron in the artist's sophistications and
skills. Many patrons had, in fact, a well-earned reputation for
discrimination and scholarship. According to Erwin Panofsky,
certain classical allegories in the work of Sir Joshua Reynolds,
which appeared meaningless to Dr. Johnson, were readily and
accurately interpreted by George III.[4] And even d'Alembert,
who as a man of the Enlightenment spoke for the autonomous
rights of the mind and against its submission to traditional
limitations, conceded that initially dependence on patronage
had freed the intellectual from "the tribunal of his rivals," that
is, of course, from his fellow writers.[5]

Generally speaking, one of the first tasks in the social interpretation of literature should be to put to rest some of the more
doctrinaire assumptions which this approach seems to invite.
For example, the tie between a given social setting and its intellectual manifestations is not necessarily something easily
labeled or manifestly single-minded. To return to the case of
patronage, it would be misleading to think that the hand of
aristocratic favor had the capacity to turn all of literature into a
series of gestures of class adulation. Some writers looked at
princes and noblemen as creatures with a capacity for moral
resolution immeasurably beyond the spiritual powers of most
humans—to great men great duties and great sorrows. Others
devoted themselves to the formalized idealization of the game
of love, a subject which provided so much of the literary stimulation for the fashionable salon. What made aristocratic literature "aristocratic" was not any one subject or aesthetic. It was
rather the capacity of this literature to reflect a milieu which, by
putting intellectual craftsmanship under the protection of tradi-

tional power, allowed the perpetuation of certain concerns of taste and imagination. One of these concerns was the careful regulation of style by an audience with leisure enough to nurse formal perfectionism. Another was the promotion of the poetic, in de Tocqueville's sense: a suggestion of the marvelous and the remote which flowed from two social characteristics of the aristocratic world—an inscrutable reverence for the past and the awe-inspiring personal and spiritual distance kept by the aristocrat himself.[6]

If certain forms of social protection do not condemn the writer to a stereotyped psychological and sociological language, the same is true of certain forms of social insecurity. The anger which modern literary intellectuals address so publicly and so pitilessly to so many features of their society is, in many ways, a special case, for we do not find at an earlier day that personal predicament leads unavoidably to large ideological quarrels. There are the classic examples of Corneille and Racine. Corneille was a provincial barrister and a reluctant courtier in an age which sometimes made elegance the synonym of literature. Racine was a well-rewarded royal favorite, adept at the palace manner and the recipient of a number of distinguished sinecures. They were both faced with public difficulties which contrasted ironically with their different dispositions. Corneille was obliged to subject his great masterpiece, *Le Cid,* to the scrutiny of the French Academy, a company of quasiofficial pundits whose competence and motivations he suspected. Racine, for all his courtly traffic, managed to incur the displeasure of his patron, the king, through careless political remarks. But neither of these uncomfortable episodes led Corneille or Racine to revise their social ideals or to pit themselves against the social order of their day. Least of all did their difficulties cause them to renounce royal or aristocratic favor, which they continued to gratefully enjoy all their lives.

We must, then, restate the fact that the self-conception, as well as the expectations and problems, of the modern writer, were the product of revolutionary changes. But revolutions do not leap into historical reality out of a Mephistophelian cloud. The social environment and content of French literature had been changing since the middle of the eighteenth century, and intellectuals had been searching for a new place and function ever since French society began to disengage itself from its traditional order. Already in the closing years of the Old Regime, the playwright Pierre Beaumarchais had challenged the "inexplicable supremacy" of those court officials who presumed to "treat on equal terms with genius" and to dictate the terms of the author's relationship with the public.[7] He had in mind, no doubt, the interference of court censors with the theater, one form of literature which offered the writer an independent, paying audience. Nevertheless, his complaint also anticipates that hoped-for later dispensation—an autonomous and inviolable author working for a free and responsible audience—which we find acclaimed in Victor Hugo's preface to *Lucrezia Borgia:*

When one sees this enlightened populace which has turned Paris into the key city of progress and which fills the theater every night, one should realize that the theater is a tribune, the theater is a pulpit.[8]

This statement rings all too evidently with the populistic forensics of a time which sometimes liked to look at history as the virtuous effluence of mass energies. It is also not easily separable from that loftiness which the office of literature acquired in the eyes of its nineteenth-century practitioners and which Hugo could not always distinguish from his own self-esteem. But, either because of or despite these sentiments, we can say that it expresses the ideal partnership between the modern writer and the modern public. As it turned out, however, this was largely a wasted hope. If there is a dominant strand in the literature of the Orleanist period, it is not Hugo's democratic optimism, but the wounded rancor at democratic betrayal found in de Vigny's *Chatterton,* a drama whose hero (or victim) is typically the young poet pushed to self-destruction by the blindness of a democratic public to the needs of the artist.[9]

The point of Chatterton's tragedy in an intellectual and a human sense was a paradox which somehow accompanied the writer's expectations and demands of recognition and which de Vigny and others of his generation came to regard as self-evident. The literary artist belonged to "the special race of inspired men," and the gift which he made to society could only be fashioned in separateness from society. He was the vessel of values which were not of the many but which they must acknowledge and extol.

In more secular language, what Chatterton's dilemma meant was that, although writers and artists had been among those socially emancipated by a revolutionary age, the novel opportunities they had thereby acquired could not be extricated from certain problems. For example, an absence of obligation to the standards of a specific social environment had made originality not only a possibility but also, in a sense, the sole point and foundation of literary creation. Yet, lacking a common heritage, the new general audience offered no distinct invitation or sounding board to the creative powers of the writer. The freedom to experiment with new artistic manners and subjects fostered in him a widened sense of self-importance and a freshly aroused sense of self-discovery, but the world whose very facelessness made this possible also made him doubtful and hesitant. This was aggravated by the simple but pervasive fact that, as a free profession, literature had to be paid for in the currency of the market. Thus, while one aspect of the new literary order made intellectual autonomy an ideal, the other made impersonal economic dependence inevitable. The anxiety and rankling contradictions of this situation bred in many writers a tendency to grow touchy concerning the momentousness and dignity of their trade, and one after another fell to speaking reverentially of the natural gap between the creator and the layman, between the imposing reach of the literary spirit and the small-minded tyranny of social demands.

Neither literary honor as such nor literature for a fee had been unknown in the past.[10] But one must recognize something new in the fervor and awe with which modern intellectual pride surrounded intimate values, thereby making market rewards morally and ideologically odious even when writers only too obviously craved them and enjoyed the luxuries that they could buy.* Success simply did not appease the nineteenth-century writer or make him less prone to hector or lecture the public on his special claims. The war (which we assume to be normal in the contemporary world) had been joined between the individualized creator and the anonymous reader—between the writer and society.

By the very nature of the contradictory challenges to which he was exposed, the writer was both overstimulated and depressed in large degrees. One of the things he had learned from the great social changes which preceded and surrounded him was the fact of his isolation. But another was that the world had become uniquely vulnerable to the power of thought and that public values could be established and pulled down by men of singular gifts. The best example of this was, of course, the French Revolution itself and the vast political and ideological mobilization that followed it. "Revolutions," wrote Regnault, "have proclaimed the reign of intelligence." [11] And Chalamel observed that the writers of the 1830's assumed that "everything is permitted to men of intelligence." [12] The deification of Rousseau and Marat (whose heart was kept in a vase hung from the ceiling of the Jacobin Club) were early instances of the cult of intelligence, and Napoléon, its supreme mani-

---

* It is only by returning to the history of this state of mind that we can understand how an eminently successful author like John Steinbeck, whose books have earned him an existence far above that of most Americans in comfort and personal freedom, can still say that in the United States writers are considered "just below acrobats and just above seals." *A Russian Journal* (New York: Viking Press, 1948), p. 27.

festation. It is important to remember that there was a purely intellectual as well as a military and political version of the Napoleonic legend. The young teacher in *The Red and the Black* carried Napoléon's portrait in his traveling case. Mrs. Trollope saw students of the *École polytechnique* strolling on Sundays with the right hand held inside the coat and a hairlock combed over the forehead.[13] For the men of ideas, Bonaparte represented the trust in their own endowment and the promise of their ambitions, the capacity of genius to rise magically from nothing to the heights of power. It was a vision which held Stendhal's loyalty for a lifetime and caused Balzac to say that he wanted to accomplish with the pen what Napoléon had gained by the sword.[14]

There are two historical views of literature and art which a sociologist must avoid. One is the "sociological" theory which fails to define clearly enough the relationship between social context and literary content. The other is the orthodox history of ideas which looks on thought as an independent historical process. An example of the first is Jean-Paul Sartre's explanation of the character of nineteenth-century literature. According to him the post-revolutionary French writer represented a case of class ideology's surviving class structure. Though the pre-revolutionary writer had been psychologically aristocratized by prolonged service to the elite, he was also a bourgeois by origin, and it would have been logical for him to return to his own class for approval and status when this class became the dominant force in French society. This did not happen, Sartre says, for two reasons. Writers carried into the new era an old definition of their craft as a pure art, free of any obligations to the daily world. The bourgeoisie, however, no matter how oppressive of other classes, was far from parasitic. It exploited, but it also worked hard and, therefore, could hardly be expected to become the sponsor of a literary art dedicated to "values" and indifferent to social tasks and interests.[15]

There is general truth in this argument, but unfortunately

also a failure to take certain important facts into account. Sartre tells us, for example, that nineteenth-century writers found it intolerable to re-enter the bourgeoisie because the bourgeoisie embodied the spirit of social pragmatism, and the idea of utility was abhorrent to the artistic tradition. Yet, the kind of aristocratic life celebrated by nineteenth-century writers was not so much that of the courtier and of the taste and decorum of the classical period as that of an earlier barony, more primitive and more warlike. Sartre fails also to make the distinction between the nonutilitarian posture of leisure-class culture, with which the intellectuals had been associated in the past, and the passionate proprietorship of beauty claimed by the intellectuals when they themselves became the cultural leaders of society. Aristocratic art was not "social" in that it was not intended to serve some public purpose or gratify a vast audience. But it remained class art even though it idealized class tastes into universal values. The great difference between this and the artistic doctrines created for and by the intellectuals is that these spoke of art and no more. It was not until the nineteenth century that the artist's art was created—the art of a new classless caste, the "pure" art of a "pure" aristocracy of thought and sensitivity.

A typical (if certainly not novel) instance of the history of ideas as it applies to contemporary cultural questions may be found in the writings of the Russian philosophical essayist Nicholas Berdyaev. According to Berdyaev, the endemic sense of spiritual crisis in our world comes from the confluence of modern scientism and individualism and the rejection of the once-universal cosmology and morality of Aquinas and Dante. He names Copernicus, Descartes, and Luther as those chiefly responsible for this unfortunate revolution.[16] The chief virtue of Berdyaev's thesis is to point to an essential issue—the modern rejection of an objective model for the creative act. Its chief shortcoming (aside from an excessive trust in the unaided power of ideas) is that it tends to prove too much. A large portion of his argument—in a sense, all of it—depends on assuming that rationalism and individualism are twin historical forces although, to take one example, everything we know about nineteenth-century romanticism shows the argument to be wrong. The romantics scorned science and rationality, but they did not necessarily return to a genuine traditionalism, either as an intellectual effort to restore an integrated community or in the practice of a confessional religion.* There was a great deal of psychological medievalism in romantic writing, of course, but chiefly as a re-enactment of the nostalgic drama of the past, with its colorful complexity and ritual splendor. As men, however, the romantics remained as individualistic and independent of a public faith as any rationalist or empiricist, and, in a deeper sense, more so. The philosophical revolution of the eighteenth century had led to the construction of political utopias, social moralities, and a general psychology, whereas literary romanticism often dedicated itself to the idiosyncratic celebration of personality.

Since the question of patronage is so basic to the traditional position of the writer, it is important that we look at its history and origins. A tradition of literary sponsorship among the hereditary and political elite of France did not really develop until the seventeenth century. Before that time, according to d'Alembert, the aristocrats had been distinguished "by a natural penchant for ignorance," and, if they purchased intellectual instruction or amusement, they were careful to keep the dispensers of these services in their place.[17] Jean de la Bruyère, for example, lived in the household of the Prince of Condé as a near-domestic, and many artists were not allowed

---

* This was true, however, of political romanticism, as opposed to literary romanticism with which it shared certain *philosophical,* but not *sociological,* premises. Political romanticism should not be confused with the so-called social romanticism. This is a misnomer sometimes applied to Saint-Simonianism, Fourierism, and other doctrines which may have been utopian, but which were decisively rationalistic in their philosophic foundations.

in fashionable places except as performers. All this changed, however, with the revolution in taste and intellectual promotion brought about by the court of Louis XIV. The housing and financing of artists and writers became an object of honorific emulation. Italian painters and sculptors were imported wholesale, lodged in Versailles, and handed letters of naturalization. A pension system was instituted. Racine was made royal historian, and Corneille was given constant favors in spite of his title of "royal upholsterer," which suggests, if only symbolically, a vestigial condition of servitude. Royal patronage declined after the death of the Sun King, but private patronage carried on in its place. By the middle of the eighteenth century, writers had become one of the chief ornaments of the sophisticated upper class and the aristocratized bourgeoisie. "An interest in letters," wrote Duclos, "has become commonplace in elegant social circles. It blurs social conditions in spite of the pride of birth and the etiquette of high station." [18]

However, Duclos' gratified assessment of the social state of literature should be read more as an indication of the writer's acquired aristocracy of taste than of his actual absorption into the ruling classes. A more realistic picture of the privileges open to writers and the distances they were required to keep emerges from the history of the French Academy, an institution which had much to do with the public ranking of scholars and men of letters. It had been decided at the foundation of the Academy in 1634 that no class distinctions were to be made among its members as academicians and that "whoever shall preside shall keep good order in the meeting as strictly and civilly as possible and in a manner befitting equals." [19] Yet, for all their civilized friendliness toward the arts, some highborn members found it difficult to live with such a liberal stipulation. An incident typical of this peculiar issue was created in 1753 by the election of the Count of Claremont, who insisted on being inducted into the Academy with the honors due to his title. The Academicians reacted with an air of tactful surprise, intimating that the count was humorlessly and, above all, needlessly out of order. The quarrel, they said, was an empty one, because noblemen had "real and personal" power which everyone was bound to honor. Academics had only intellectual dignity, but this, however, they would not surrender "for all the pensions in the world." [20] It is clear, then, that what men of letters demanded was not social equality but occupational self-esteem. But one should add to this, that, for all the discretion and propriety with which they were made, the claims of academics were far from trivial in a society where a most intricate system of domestic customs allowed books to circulate freely as honorific objects and where art and learning had been made a matter of state policy. It is one of the most glorious signs of the happiness of a state, Louis XIV had said on granting the Academy its original charter, "that Science and Art should flourish in it and that Letters be held in honor as well as Arms, since they are one of the chief instruments of virtue." [21]

We see from this proclamation to what degree Louis XIV or his advisers were mindful of the classic doctrine which granted literature a social title, not only as a public article of aesthetic luxury, but also as a vehicle of moral excellence. The second of these attributes should always be remembered in considering classical literature. For Molière, the duty of comedy was "to correct men while diverting them," and, for Le Bossu, "to give moral instruction under the allegory of action." More grandly still, Vossius said of poets that they were "physicians of manners." [22] These were not mere abstractions or pious didactics, but part of a convention which used aesthetic and moral prescriptions as a bolster to social sentiment. Let us take, for instance, La Mesnadière's admonition to poets that they must avoid dealing with "the meanness of avarice, the infamy of indulgence, the horror of cruelty, the smell of poverty." [23] At first, the coupling of a degraded economic condition with a series of moral aberrations seems unexpectedly arbitrary. Yet, what La Mesnadière suggests is that social distances must be regarded as

an index of spiritual qualities and that moral dignity naturally
emanates from certain untouched social heights (that is, the
aristocracy) which serve it as model and embodiment. It is only
from a point of view such as this that we can understand how,
in analyzing the epic passions of tribal Greece by the courtly
standards of royal France, Fénelon was led to the conclusion
that Homer's gods and heroes were "unworthy of that idea that
we have of a gentleman." [24] In other words, the classical ideal
had a universal rhetoric and a class aim. It sought above all *la
belle nature,* the most elevated possibilities of the human character beyond the limits of passion. But the creature in which
this essence lived and breathed was the civilized gentleman,
educated in the classics and trained in propriety—a graceful
monument to poise, taste, and learning.

At its worst, aristocratic art was guilty of a frivolous appetite
for manneristic delights or, as Malézieu put it, "toiling in the
galleys of sophistication." In addition to coining such painfully
demure figures of speech, Malézieu was also the chief cultural entertainer of the Duchess of Maine (Voltaire's patron-
ess) and the inventor of a literary parlor game which required
players to write a poem dictated by an initial letter drawn in a
lottery. Those who drew an "O" wrote an ode, and those who
drew an "A," an apotheosis.[25] One of the clearest examples of
the class bias of traditional taste can be seen in the revealing
narrowness with which Voltaire looked on Shakespearean
drama. Voltaire granted that there was an element of the "great
and terrible," even the sublime, in Shakespeare's writing. But
he professed incomprehension and astonishment in the face of
what he regarded as Shakespeare's barbaric eccentricities. More
significantly still, he thought these not merely aesthetic flaws
but social sins. How could Shakespeare (in *Hamlet*) allow
gravediggers on the stage who actually dug a grave while
"singing and drinking at their work, and passing the low jokes
common to this sort of people" or (in *Julius Caesar*) put before an audience "the idle jests of Roman shoemakers and

cobblers"? [26] This link in Voltaire's mind between what was artistically legitimate and what was socially proper can be seen quite explicitly in his comparison of Shakespeare and Racine. At the beginning of Racine's *Iphigénie,* Agamemnon says that "all is asleep, the army, the winds, even Neptune." In the opening scene of *Hamlet,* when an officer questions a soldier about his watch, the soldier answers; "Not a mouse stirs." A soldier might talk that way in the guardhouse, says a tried Voltaire, but not on the stage before "the first persons of the nation," who spoke among themselves in a noble language and to whom the author should address himself in the same manner. [27]

Because it has been my purpose here to present two general worlds of literary value and literary personality, the classical and the contemporary, this chapter and others compare directly the literatures of the *Ancien Régime* and of the nineteenth century and ignore, conveniently and inevitably, the more complex historical facts. Classicism, of course, did not reign undefiled up to the end of the old days. Diderot's aesthetics, written in the 1730's, seem, on paper at least, like the incarnation of modern popular melodrama. His *Rameau's Nephew* has been claimed as an ancestor of the nineteenth-century Bohemians. Intimacy, subjectivity, incidental realism can all be found in the middle-class novel and drama of the eighteenth century. We can also find at that time clear signs of the struggle to establish the intellectual as an independent social figure. This was, in fact, the subject of a long *Essay on the Relations of Noblemen and Men of Letters* by the scientist and philosopher Jean d'Alembert, who wrote it both as a short sociology of the traditional literary household and as a manifesto calling for the end of the old partnership between rank and intelligence. The *Essay* begins with some generalizations which seem to echo obliquely the view of society as a system of separate rights and obligations. When d'Alembert asks equality for the writer, it is not as a share of some general human property—men as men are not equal and never will be, he

says—but as a privilege which the writer uniquely earns
through his work. He concedes that noblemen had done literature a service by turning it into an occupation under their
beneficence. And he has enough of the old taste for leisurely
intellectual exploration to say that the company of a sophisticated aristocrat, respectful of the writer's gifts, was the "most
useful and noble association which a thinking man can have." [28]
Nevertheless, the analytical impetus and the rising intellectual
self-confidence of the Encyclopaedic generation carried d'Alembert beyond this point and into a critique of the psychological
discomfort and cultural blight which social convention could
impose. Aristocrats might be swept sometimes by the "sponsorship compulsion" (*fureur de protéger*), but they could not always free themselves from a view of the writer as a sumptuary
hobby, a glittering but inferior possession. This meant the constant presence of a cramping and distracting strain in the world
of sponsored literature, not only for the writer but for the
patron himself, since the prestige value of sponsorship stemmed
precisely from the fashionable contemporary glorification of
"the lights." [29]

D'Alembert classified intellectuals who accepted these conditions into three kinds: slaves unaware of their own slavery and,
therefore, incurable; struggling, weak men who resolved to
be free in the morning and slipped back into servitude in the
evening; and, most culpable, apologetic deceivers who dis-
credited their masters in private and eulogized them in public.
He was sensitive to the oppressive ambivalence of the intellectuals' position and to their craving for personalized recognition. He spoke of the trying familiarities of the nobility which
burdened the writer with the need to be tactfully reticent,
because he never knew whether they represented a genuine
egalitarian gesture or a patronizing game. D'Alembert thought
that the aristocrats of his time were being educated for social
polish and amenities and could no longer claim a superior

education which made them the natural judges of art, learning, or men. He was deeply annoyed and humiliated by having to pay court to "useless nullities whose scandalous luxury is an insult to the public." [30] Men of letters, he said, had at least as much right to opulence as noblemen. Certainly they had no duty to be poor. On the other hand, they owed it to themselves to endure poverty for the sake of those things which were their duty: independence and truth. In the end he found himself advocating the revolutionary principles of personal intellectual honor and the career open to talent. Three things separated men; virtue, money, and intelligence; but only the last could be regarded as objective and, for that reason, legitimate. A writer might be willing to offer a gentleman the courtesies to which he was accustomed only if he were to get in return that "more real" respect which was owed to the mind. Rank, he wrote, clearly drawing a fond distinction, is the source of deference; intelligence is the source of esteem.[31]

D'Alembert had compared the intellectual work of his time to "a river which had burst its dams [and] . . . everything along with it that stood in its way." [32] And the nineteenth century inherited both his conviction and the novel doctrines of privilege which accompanied it. This was true of poets and artists as well as social philosophers and planners. Henri de Saint-Simon, for example, wanted to divide society into classes, the first of them ("to which," he said, "I have the honor of belonging") to be made up of scientists, artists and men of ideas.[33] But it is perhaps among the literary figures that the largest implications of this new self-regard are to be found, both as an impetus to artistic creation and as a guide to life. The situation is in some ways reminiscent of the Renaissance scholars who, after losing or renouncing the sponsorship of church and community which had furnished them with the social and institutional basis for a universalistic style of thinking, were, in fact, forced to become universal themselves and to make God proclaim the moral and intellectual greatness of Man. This is the way He speaks in one of the most celebrated of the Renaissance documents, Pico della Mirandola's *Oration:*

> We have set thee at the world's center . . . so that with freedom of choice and with honor, as though maker and molder of thyself in whatever shape thou shalt prefer. Thou shalt have the power to degenerate into the lower forms of life, which are brutish. Thou shalt have the power, out of thy soul's judgment, to be reborn into higher forms, which are divine.[34]

The nineteenth century, however, went much further, overcoming both the need for moral self-justification and the classical virtues of taste and form. Genius was unleashed as an all-powerful, radical, and unequaled event, a gift of nature which must be allowed to take its course no matter how disruptive to common perceptions. It was now not only the right of intelligence to be respected, but also the duty of genius to tear up norms, to shatter the confines of rule and to permit a whole new world of reality, uniquely perceived, conceived, and expressed, to emerge out of its oceanic depths. Sigmund Freud says that, in the modern world, explanation of historical events tends to appeal to impersonal forces—economic relationships, food supply, technology, climate, or population—rather than to the energies of the personal hero found in ancient mythology.[35] Alexis de Tocqueville, who also believed this distinction to be true, thought it peculiar to the imagination of an egalitarian age which could only accept collective motivations as decisive.[36] But when we look at the literature of the nineteenth century it is not an exaggeration to say that, faced with the advent of the democratic public and the opening of society to democratic impulses, men of letters reacted by returning intellectual acts to a mythical atmosphere. Artistic and literary creation became something formidable, awesome, surrounded by an aura of trance and revelation. To fall into melodramatic ecstasy or thunderstruck speechlessness in the presence of a great mind became the most fashionable intellectual mannerism of the period. Heine tells us how, on his way to visit Goethe for the first time, he carefully rehearsed what he thought was a notably suitable speech for greeting the Master, and how, when he was finally received, all he could mumble was, "The prune trees along the road from Jena to Weimar give excellent prunes for quenching thirst." It was in an agony of forced resolution that Théophile Gautier first knocked on Victor Hugo's door:

I had sat down on the steps, he relates, for my legs refused to carry me any further, when suddenly the door opened and, in the midst of a blaze of light, as Phoebus and Apollo came forward through the gates of dawn, there appeared on the dark landing Victor Hugo himself in his glory. Like Esther before Ahasuerus, I nearly fainted.[37]

In the language of Max Weber's sociology of ideas, literary activity had changed from "traditional" to "charismatic." That is, it had become an "intimate task" carried out publicly by the subject of a "mana attack." [38] One can almost say that the new ideal of literary invention was a kind of psychological translation of the idea of genesis, of creation out of nothing or out of the creator himself. To be sure there were other images of literary leadership. One of them might be called, after Flaubert, the mandarin principle. Personal in its foundation, it was more formal and normative than that of the charismatic creator and dedicated rather to a perfection of psychological detachment and a preciseness of language. Groups like the Saint-Simonians, who were committed to organized social action, held a "team" view of the intellect and always referred to complementary groups of specialists, artists, and professionals who were to work together as tutors of society. But of all these versions of intellectual gifts and powers, the most dominant and the most dramatic was that of the "mythical-individual" poet found in the literary manifestos of Victor Hugo. In the preface to *Hernani,* Hugo wrote:

Tear down theory, poetic systems. . . . No more rules, no more
models. . . . Genius conjures up rather than learns. . . . For talent to surrender. . . . personal originality. . . . would be like for
God to become a lackey.[39]

In the *Odes et Ballades,* he described the poet's inspiration and
its public impact in this way:

> An overwhelming force breaks forth
> Through his mind.
> He is as though suspended.
> And suddenly, as if launched by lightning,
> His words light up like fire.
> Men prostrated, surround this mysterious Sinai.
> Thunderbolts crown his head.
> His forehead bears a god.[40]

Saint-Simon warned the ruling classes that they had no choice but
to endow the work of intellectuals with money and "great prestige." Otherwise they would be forced to do so by men of genius who had in their hand the "sceptre of public opinion." [41]
Saint-Simon is reported to have said on his deathbed that a party
of the workers would come into existence "forty-eight hours"
after the appearance of the second Saint-Simonian publication.[42]
An unnamed prophet who, at the Paris Opera in 1841, distributed pamphlets proclaiming the new law of love and justice
(typically his "action" program consisted of winning over poets,
princes, novelists, ministers, and artists), was certain that "the
sun of intelligence was flooding the horizon." With more tri-
umphant confidence still, he predicted: "Fifteen days of con-
scientious study and you shall see." [43] With his customary air of
fiat lux Hugo stated that the function of the poet was to change
charity to fraternity, laziness to utility, iniquity to justice, the
crowd to a people, the mob to a nation, the nations to humanity,
and war to love.[44]   It should be clear from all this that the
belief, not only in the virtue, but in the power of ideas depended
and, to some degree, fed itself upon the freedom from class obligations. Once the intellectuals were compelled to trust ideas

alone and to see themselves as creatures of large and articulate intentions looking upon all of life, it became an article of faith to them that, if only ideas were properly organized, distributed and listened to, an intellectual task force might actually transform society. But as it happens, the blessings of this freedom turned out to be inextricable from its anxieties. Because of his detachment, the writer had to make the self the center of all meaning and, armed with this self, face a social world which was now, in fact, all of society. Hence, the tone of Hugo's pronouncements, which are at the same time egotistical and socially programmatic. This, however, was the optimistic face of intellectual Bonapartism. The other side of it was, as we know, plagued by a chronic mixture of suspicion, anger, and contempt, bred of the uncertain connection with a social milieu that appeared distant, unformed, and frequently hostile. This explains the never-resolved two-sidedness of literary attitudes during this period. Arrogance and almost utopian self-confidence on the one hand; fear, impotence and martyrdom on the other.

Not surprisingly we find this ambivalence translating itself and being translated into the concrete conditions of literary merchandising. Modern literature was a venture that could pay off handsomely or turn into a total loss. A "hit" on the market could make a reputation. Some reputations did not get made at all. Of course, this could happen in business or the professions. But there was a major ideological and psychological difference between literature and other forms of productivity which made failure particularly painful; namely, the exalted view which writers held of their calling. The response to this situation in personality terms is described in Louis Culmer's portrait of the modern man of letters,

> . . . an angel, a demon, beautiful and ugly, base and sublime, proud and servile, humble and wrathful, sensible and extravagant, menacing and submissive, slave and tyrant.[45]

This profile represents more than the mere annoyance and confusion of a businesslike editor before the colorful but vexatious unpredictability of literary people. It is actually the behavior outline of a person who is deeply self-centered and self-sanctioned, but who is also dependent for success on the uncertain verdict of the outside world. The point is made quite clear when Culmer tells us that the change from the angelic to the demonic and from servility to dictatorial overbearance are really the "before" and "after" phases of literary victory.[46] Even the money-hardened Balzac, who it was said speculated on how much money his love letters might be worth, defended intellectual property not as a commercial right, but as a unique title derived from spiritual sources.

If there is in the world a sacred property, if there is something that belongs to man, is it not that which man creates between heaven and earth, that which has no root other than intelligence? [47]

It was an inescapably ambiguous predicament. The claims of the dispenser of intellectual values were always made to rest on the contention that these were higher things which could not be rendered into utilitarian terms. And yet, of course, the pragmatic point of the writer's demand on the public was to obtain a predictable rate of reward for his work. Consequently, when writers complained about social negligence and misunderstanding, they put themselves in the curious position of decrying the lack of appreciation of the inherent value of literary creation because of the absence of material remuneration for it. However, all ambiguity vanished when writers spoke of their ideal social function. Here the literary man was always the protagonist of a mission, of a "holy task," [48] as Hugo put it, and it is clear from many sources that, not only professionals, but all sorts of literary debutants and volunteers in the ranks of the intellectual proletariat took it upon themselves to display the esoteric pride and solemn talk which such a belief was bound to promote. This is what Thackeray wrote after visiting Paris in the 1830's:

. . . [T]here is scarcely a beggarly beardless scribbler of words of poems or prose, but tells you in his preface of the *sainteté* of the *sacerdoce littéraire;* or a dirty student sucking his tobacco and beer, and reeling home with a grisette . . . who is not convinced of the necessity of a new "Messianism," and will not hiccup, to such as will listen, chapters of his own drunken Apocalypse.[49]

What this statement shows is that the tension between the heroic self-image of the creative person and the impersonal commercialization of the market had become a social phenomenon, a manner adopted by the self-appointed man of literary parts and the vicarious protagonist of literary struggles. Unquestionably, such an epochal concept of literature helped many a young man make his occupational shortcoming "significant" and to call himself a casualty in the battle for "values," while otherwise he might have been an ordinary failure. But it is just as true to say that the sufferings which these young men were willing to endure for the sake of sensitivity, the glory of genius, and the rights of beauty were in themselves real enough.

NOTES TO CHAPTER V

1. Cited in Levin L. Schücking, *The Sociology of Literary Taste* (London: Routledge & Kegan Paul, 1950), p. 10.

2. Cited in Alan Moorehead, "The Angel of May," *The New Yorker,* February 24, 1951, p. 35.

3. Schücking, *op. cit.,* p. 22.

4. Erwin Panofsky, *Meaning in the Visual Arts* (New York: Doubleday Anchor Books, 1955), p. 295.

5. Jean d'Alembert, "Essai sur la société des gens de lettres et les grands." *Oeuvres complètes* (5 vols.; Paris: A. Belin, 1822), IV, 340.

6. Alexis de Tocqueville, *Democracy in America,,* II, 48-52, 55-60, 72-76.

7. Helen Simpson, *op. cit.,* p. 58.

8. Hugo, *Oeuvres complètes* (2 vols.; Paris: 1845), II, 8.

9. Alfred de Vigny, *Oeuvres complètes* (9 vols.; Paris: Delagrave),

VIII-IX, 14-15. De Vigny classifies intellectuals into three groups: men of letters, great writers, and poets. They have different characteristics and enjoy different degrees of success and repute. What he calls "men of letters" comprise the rhetorician, the publicist, and the respectable hack—the pleasers of crowds, the "amiable kings of the moment." The "great writers" are, in effect, the great critics, men of superior and exacting analytical powers, representative of "the genius [of] scrutiny carried to the highest degree." Although they are always under attack they are also granted the respect of their adversaries. They are public personages. Unlike the poet, neither "men of letters" nor "great writers" are to be pitied. The poet, on the other hand, because of his spiritual nature, is the particular victim of public neglect, a neglect he finds uniquely impossible to endure.

In spite of these distinctions and of the special plight which de Vigny attributes to the poet, it is perfectly legitimate to refer to de Vigny's discussion as typifying the isolated intellectual because what he says of the poet is said by others—novelists, critics, essayists—as generally true of the literary profession.

10. Diderot in his young days wrote perfume advertising and sermons for laggard priests. Business—show business—was certainly a consideration with Molière. The Turkish ballet and Grand Mama-muchi scene in the *Bourgeois gentilhomme* was deliberately introduced as an exploitation of the Oriental fashion of the moment. He wrote *Don Juan* in prose and at great speed because the theme was a money-making one and several companies were competing for it. Albert Guerard, *Art for Art's Sake* (Boston: Lothrop, Lees & Shepard Co., 1936), pp. 106-108.

11. Cited in *Les Français, op. cit.*, **VIII**, 232.

12. Cited in Orlo Williams, *op. cit.*, p. 114.

13. Frances Trollope, *op. cit.*, p. 148.

14. Louis Maigron, *Le Romantisme et les moeurs* (Paris: Honoré Champion, 1910), p. 77.

15. Jean-Paul Sartre, *Baudelaire*, trans. Martin Turnell (Paris: Librairie Gallimard, 1950), pp. 137-139.

16. Nicholas Berdyaev, *Solitude and Society* (London: Geoffry Bless, The Centenary Press, 1938), p. 99. Berdyaev refers specifically to romanticism. In his treatment, however, as in that of other writers—Bertrand Russell and Irving Babbitt, for instance—it is almost impossible to distinguish between romanticism and the modern intellect.

17. Jean d'Alembert, *op. cit.*, p. 338.

18. Cited in Marguerite Glotz & Madeleine Marie, *Salons du XVIII siècle* (Paris: Nouvelles Éditions Latines, 1949), p. 20.

19. Cited in D. Maclaren Robertson, *A History of the French Academy* (New York: G. W. Dillingham Co., 1910), p. 12. See also Frederic Masson, *L'Academie française* (Paris: Paul Ollendorf, 1912), p. 11 *et seq.*

20. Cited in Maclaren Robertson, *op. cit.*, pp. 97-99.

21. *Ibid.*, pp. 20-21.

22. Cited in René Wellek, *A History of Modern Criticism* (2 vols.; New Haven: Yale University Press, 1955), I, 16, 21.

23. *Loc. cit.*

24. *Loc. cit.*

25. Marguerite Glotz & Madeleine Marie, *op. cit.*, p. 66.

26. Voltaire, *Works,* Tobias Smollet, ed.; trans. William F. Fleming (42 vols.; Paris: E. R. Dumont, 1901), XXXIX, 45-46.

27. Cited in René Wellek, *op. cit.*, p. 36.

28. Jean d'Alembert, *op. cit.*, p. 359.

29. *Ibid.*, pp. 362, 358, 360.

30. *Ibid.*, pp. 356-357, 368.

31. *Ibid.*, pp. 353-354.

32. Cited in Ernst Cassirer, *The Philosophy of Enlightenment* (Boston: The Beacon Press, 1952), p. 32.

33. Henri Comte de Saint-Simon, *Selected Writings,* F. M. H. Markham, ed. and trans., (New York: Macmillan Co., 1952), p. 2.

34. Pico della Mirandola, "Oration on the Dignity of Man" in Ernst Cassirer *et al., The Renaissance Philosophy of Man* (Chicago: The University Press, 1948), p. 225. See also Alfred Von Martin, *Sociology of the Renaissance* (London: Kegan Paul, Trench, Trubner & Co., 1944), p. 53 *et seq.,* and Charles Trinkhaus, *Adversity's Noblemen* (London: P. S. King and Sons, 1940).

35. Sigmund Freud, *Moses and Monotheism* (New York: Vintage books, 1955), p. 136.

36. Alexis de Tocqueville, *Democracy in America,* II, 85-88.

37. Théophile Gautier, *Histoire du romantisme* (Paris: Bibliothèque Charpentiere, 1874), pp. 10-11.

38. Max Weber, *Wirtschaft und Gesellschaft* (2 vols.; Tubingen: Mohr, 1956), II, 662.

39. Victor Hugo, *Oeuvres complètes,* I, 162-163.

40. *Ibid.*, II, 495.

41. Saint-Simon, *op. cit.*, pp. 1-3.

42. Cited in Edmund Wilson, *To the Finland Station* (Garden City, New York: Doubleday Anchor Books, 1953), p. 85.

43. Cited in Jules Bertaut, *op. cit.*, p. 360.

44. René Wellek, *op. cit.*, II, 256.

45. *Les Français,* III, 222.

46. *Ibid.*, p. 222.

47. Cited in Jules Bertaut, *op. cit.*, pp. 111-112.

48. Frances Trollope, *op. cit.*, p. 101.

49. William M. Thackeray, *op. cit.*, p. 302.

CHAPTER VI

THE LITERARY VIEW
OF BOURGEOIS SOCIETY

THE TRADITIONAL French middle class had, as we know, kept certain important distinctions between the old bourgeois and the newly rich, between the shopkeeper and the *haute bourgeois,* who lived as splendidly as the nobleman. But from merchants to intellectuals, lawyers, and bureaucrats, the middle class was a commanding social force in France toward the end of the eighteenth century,* and nearly everyone agrees now that the events of the French Revolution merely set the seal of political power upon its long historical ascent.

If this is so, why did the literati wait until the nineteenth

---

* Mixing truth with exaggeration, Aynard remarks that Voltaire was not only the last bourgeois to be caned by the aristocracy but also the first to be embraced by them as a friend among equals. He refers to the famous episode of the Chevalier de Rohan. When, in the course of a disagreement, de Rohan insulted Voltaire, the latter, refusing a commoner's forbearance, traded vilifications with him. In return de Rohan had Voltaire caned by his servants while he looked on. Voltaire was at that time thirty years old.

century before launching a cultural assault on the middle class? The answer is that not until then did the middle class appear as a cultural menace to the professional protagonists of spiritual interests. The bourgeoisie had risen through its customary dedication to self-improvement and market efficiency. But while these virtues made it powerful, it did not make it self-assured. For, after reaching a certain eminence, it always turned to the cultural props of the aristocracy as a means of overcoming the homeliness and provinciality of outlook which tradition regarded as the taint of the middle-class soul. In spite of its triumphs, therefore, the bourgeoisie had not been able to produce a style of life capable of commanding universal admiration— that is to say, of setting the standards of cultural achievement and etiquette for the society as a whole. However, with the destruction of the aristocracy by the Revolution, France witnessed also the liquidation of the Old Regime's spiritual apparatus. And this, and the social changes that followed, allowed the historical middle-class traits of calculation and pragmatism to assert themselves, not only as an unmixed way of life, but as a dominant one.

In a short but impatient essay Benedetto Croce once argued against what he called the purely polemic use of the term "bourgeois," that is, with no purpose other than to speak of a human type and a historical era whose every moral and psychological feature was dismissed as either contemptible or grotesque.[1] Yet considering only the intellectual and emotional history of the word, Croce's irritation seems surprising, for the peculiar virtue of the bourgeoisie as a concept and an image is precisely that of evoking a primary sense of likes and dislikes which causes people to align themselves on one side or another of broad cultural and social questions. In politics, for example, bourgeois has usually meant servitude to economic power and an inability to think in a vast and epochal style about historical changes and conditions. In an ethical sense, it suggests an ungenerous and stifling provincialism—that "middle-class morality" always uttered as a term of self-evident condemnation. Used to describe intellectual psychological and aesthetic characteristics, it implies a lack of reverence for creative values and the courage to act on those values in daily life. There is around the word, then, a cluster of attitudes the sharing or rejecting of which is presumed to divide modern men into separate worlds of intellectual and cultural awareness, of sensitivity and of imagination.

In any discussion of the middle class, one cannot avoid considering a doctrine which has taken as its historical task the destruction of both that class and all its principles, Marxian socialism. Marxism holds that both the character of social relations and the operation of historical law not only direct, but drive the mind toward an objective understanding of social reality. For this reason, Marxism represents a revolutionary form of rationalism which views philosophical transformation and the reordering of social life as part of the same historical process. Marx, it is true, could not quite hold to a consistent view when it came to explaining the origins of ideas and their relationship to political action. In *Capital,* for instance, he said that ideas were nothing but the material world "reflected in the human mind," and in *The German Ideology* he described "mental production" (politics, morality, religion, metaphysics, and so forth) as echoing in the language of concepts the conditions of "real" (or material) existence.[2] In *The Eighteenth Brumaire,* on the other hand, he argued that intellectual representatives of the petty bourgeoise were not, as a rule, shopkeepers or had to be, which suggests, and in effect concedes, that class ideas might be acquired through intellectual synthesis alone, without benefit of class interests or possessions.[3] And in his letters we find that bourgeois ideas, as "traditionally acquired rubbish," could be inherited even by the proletariat.[4]

To these hesitations Lenin added a footnote of plain historical realism when he said that, as a matter of fact, the laboring classes had never been able to think beyond the aims of better

pay and more comfortable working conditions and that socialism as a movement had been the creation of intellectual dis-
senters from the propertied class.[5] Marx, to be sure, never
made such an admission, but Engels did, and conferred the
honor on Marx. "We owe what we are to him," he wrote after
Marx's death, "and the movement as it is today is the creation
of his theoretical and practical work." [6] In rendering such a personal homage to Marx's historical inventiveness, Engels con-
travened the core of orthodox Marxism. And in so doing he
pointed also to the sociological irony hidden within the intellectual attack on the bourgeoisie. For whether we mean by bourgeois a psychological type, a moral and cultural atmosphere, or
a class with certain social and political interests, the history of
anti-bourgeois sentiment has been, in nearly all its forms, the
history of defectors from the middle class, who in the struggle to
live with the consequences of their secession, have worked to
create a new order worthy of their approval.

Vast and hopeful in tone, thoroughly political, and committed to the salvation of man without and within, Marxism is
the chief instance (certainly the most influential) of anti-
bourgeois thinking as a social creed. But it is only one aspect of
such a tradition. Another, what I have called "the literary revolt," has tended to be a-rationalistic—even anti-rationalistic,
essentially unmoved by politics or social promise and pledged
above all to the affirmation and defense of artistic and personal
imagination. Yet somewhat surprisingly, considering their differences on the moral and intellectual plane, there are certain
agreements between these two positions. Both believe, for instance, that there is such a thing as the bourgeois mind, and
that this mind distributes itself within certain parts of the social
body. Originally it is found in one class, but it can transmit itself to others. Marx spoke of the infection of the proletariat with
bourgeois aspirations and of the appropriation of bourgeois
ideals by intellectuals. Literary men also thought that, while the
bourgeois spirit was by and large located in the middle class, it

could communicate itself as a state of mind. In this sense, according to Victor Hugo, the bourgeoisie was simply "the contented part of the population." [7]

Beyond this point, however, great disparities begin. Literary men tended to look upon the bourgeoisie as the embodiment of triviality and gross ennervation of the mind. For Marxism, as for other forms of socialism, the bourgeoisie represented, on the contrary, a crucial stage, not only in the history of social relations, but in the organization of human intelligence. Indeed, one of the things that Marx inherited from Saint-Simonians, Fourierists, and other "utopian" socialists was a pride in rationalism, efficiency, and technology which, as an aspect of modern productivity, he applauded as zealously as the loudest progress booster. Marx also looked on the "objectivity" of human relations brought into the world by the bourgeoisie as a great scientific opportunity. Some of the early passages of *The Communist Manifesto* seem to suggest that the materialism of the bourgeoisie had affronted a regard for tradition still lingering in Marx's mind. One might even think that Marx had been shaken by the power of the middle class to drown chivalry and religion in the "icy waters of calculation," to reduce once honored professions—the law, poetry and science—to the condition of wage labor. But as we go on we find the point to be quite the opposite, namely that the middle class had achieved the destruction of social sentimentalism by substituting naked and direct exploitation for exploitation "veiled by religious and political illusion." The result, Marx thought, was to be a scientific clarification of the nature of social reality and an enlargement of rationality. Through the bourgeois revolution of social relations, man would at last be compelled "to face with sober sense his real conditions of life, and his relations with his kind." Marx was led by this conviction to some of his broadest cultural predictions. Due to the massive and international character of bourgeois economic enterprise, the countryside had, at last, been made completely dependent on the towns and, in the process, had rescued a considerable part of the population from "the idiocy of rural life." Cosmopolitanism would replace localism in material and intellectual production. Just as capitalism had become the first world-wide economic and social system, intellectual life would become, for the first time, universal.[8]

Now when we turn to literary discontent, we find nothing but flight from the scientific and rationalistic spirit celebrated by the socialists. Cathedrals were worshiped, not machinery; and even agnostic writers bewailed secularism as a threat to the sensitive apprehension of life and beauty. What the literary imagination craved was, above all, the very "veiled" relationships exposed, according to Marx, by capitalist economics. In the drama and in the novel, this was the age of medievalism, purple emotion, ancient gold, and archaic blood ties, the age of local color and the picturesque. Creatures of urban civilization that they were, the literary rebels often suspected cosmopolitanism and yearned after remote and unspoiled societies. The uniqueness of national and regional life became a stylistic and a psychological passion. So did the hatred of technology, the violator of nature's mystery and integrity, and the love of craftsmanship—a personal, intimate, subjective mode of production.

A different anti-bourgeois position meant a different characterization of the bourgeoisie itself, a different system of accusations and suspicions. For the socialists the great intellectual handicap of the bourgeois was their inability to carry the work of history beyond the limits of their own class interests. From the literary point of view the great flaw of the bourgeoisie, its great inner deformity, was a creative poverty and a cowardice of imagination natural in men who were slaves to pragmatic design. The artist, therefore, was portrayed as the fated carrier of the "instinct for the beautiful." The surrounding enemy was described as "a powerful majority, which we call bourgeois . . . schooled in the cult of the materialistic ego with no impulse other than self-preservation." [9] Materialism was only one feature of the bourgeoisie. Another was its spiritual paltriness.

Augustin Thierry wrote that it had "no taste for great enterprise," [10] and Louis Blanc that it was "too utterly devoid of grandeur to urge extreme courses." [11] Although Blanc was a deeply political man, immersed in libertarian advocacy, his words embody the essential spirit of the literary aspects of the anti-bourgeois revolt.

To many literary artists of the nineteenth century, political involvement was a matter of indifference. On the other hand, inner strife, extremes of subjective experience, and storms of personal expression were the things through which life gained its meaning. It was, in fact, this capacity of spiritual strife and force of expression that separated the creative man from the prudence and pragmatism of the bourgeoisie, that is to say, from the qualities which had given the bourgeoisie its worldly successes as well as the barrenness and tedium of its soul.

In Orleanist France, as in other countries, literary discontent was generally bred in the atmosphere of the romantic movement. The influence of romanticism on what Jacques Barzun calls "the modern ego" is, in fact, so extensive, that some intellectual historians, like Bertrand Russell, in discussing this movement find themselves discussing the whole of the contemporary outlook. Yet, nothing is so characteristic of romantic studies as haziness about the concept, its application and chronology, and the self-accommodating interpretations based on the reputed ineffability of the idea itself. It is, therefore, not surprising that, in sampling the uses of the term, Barzun should be able to list close to ninety contradictory definitions of it, among them "materialistic," "mysterious," "individualistic," "tribal," "Nordic," "Christian," "conservative," and "revolutionary." [12] Nor is it surprising that Lovejoy's seemingly exhaustive essay on the same topic should end by being a catalogue of all its possible ambiguities.[13]

Romanticism is easier to understand if looked at in terms of its conception of the individual and his relation to society. From the literary point of view (leaving for the moment the so-called political romanticism) and certainly from the point of view of French literature, the following things were true of the romantic movement:*

The ideal of self-expression. The most important purpose in life is to express oneself through creative work and to realize fully one's individuality.

The freedom of self-expression. Every law, convention, or rule which prevents self-expression or the full enjoyment of creative individual experience should be abolished or ignored.

The idea of genius.† The creative powers of the individual are essentially unexplainable; they are a fact and a gift of nature.

---

* The categories of romanticism used here have been suggested in part by Malcolm Cowley's discussion of Bohemian values (so closely allied historically with romanticism) in *Exile's Return* (New York: Viking Press, 1956), pp. 60-61.

† I agree, of course, that the idea of genius is not an invention of the romantic movement. As Wellek has pointed out, "inspiration and *furor poeticus*" were conventional phrases of the Renaissance. However, as Wellek himself tells us, this emphasis on imagination was matched by the insistence on judgment and design. As Wellek quotes Alexander Pope:

> The winged courser, like a generous horse
> Shows most true mettle when you check his course.

Wellek, *op. cit.,* **II,** 13-14. This is not true of the somewhat apocalyptic theories of creativity held by romantics like Victor Hugo (see p. 79) or Théophile Dondey, who precisely reverse Pope's image:

> Like wild horses without rider or bridle,
> Manes to the wind and fire in their eye,
> Ironic and rebellious thoughts leap about
> Within the brow of genius. (see p. 115)

In an age like the Renaissance, whose intellectual self-confidence never lost a rationalistic mold, Pico della Mirandola could maintain that it was entirely within the power of man to descend to the brutes or to rise to the angels. But since romanticism, it has been possible to hold within oneself, as Dylan Thomas claimed he did, a brute and an angel. In *La Barrière et le niveau,* Edmond Goblot's psychological-historical account of the bourgeois's presumed incurable lack of sublimity, Goblot says that they can never become angels because they are too fearful of becoming beasts. In the tradition of such literary psychology, we can understand the characteristically romantic notion that delicate and complex sentiments may be harbored within a sullen and animalistic shell—why, for example,

The rejection of general or rational causality. Every event of natural or social reality is unique and should be apprehended directly in its living singularity.

"Cosmic self-assertion." [14] The literary man is a demi-god, a natural aristocrat. He holds world-meaning in the palm of his hand and is the carrier of the higher values of civilization. Therefore, special respect is owed him and special freedom should be granted to him.

The social alienation of the literary man. Paradoxically, though men of letters are the vessels of superior values, they are denied by their fellow men, whose main interests are material gratification and the enjoyment of the cruder forms of power.

The hostility of modern society to talent and sensitivity. The modern world is sunk in vulgar contentment and driven by a materialism which is essentially trivial and inhumane—regardless of the technological complexity or institutional efficiency which may accompany it.

World-weariness and "the horror of daily life." [15] Between the creative person and the surrounding society there is always an unresolved tension. The aspirations of the creative person are such that they can never be satisfied by ordinary existence. Daily life, therefore, is a constant denial and an intolerable burden.

Romantic literature glorified strong passions, unique emotions, and special deeds. It despised normalcy, foresight, concern with customary affairs, and attention to feasible goals—everything of which the middle class was a daily example. Marx praised the bourgeoisie for its power to objectify the world. Literary men decried it for the same reason, seeing in this power a chill, analytical obsessiveness which would destroy the integrity of human experience, not only intellectually but psychologically. Romantic philosophers warned against the spirit of measurement because of what it did to human knowledge, splitting it into isolated parts.

The aesthetic rebels pointed to what it did to the human personality by draining it of stature and vitality for the sake of quantitative gain. The bourgeoisie represented ambition without passion, possessiveness without depth of desire, power

---

behind the bestial gruntings of a loathsome creature like Hugo's hunchback, Quasimodo, there lies a hidden sensibility waiting to be discovered.

without grandeur, everything that was spiritually paltry and anti-vital, everything that was inadequate and pettily self-protective, in a psychological and even a biological way. Greed was bourgeois, but so were carpet slippers and head colds.

From different moral and intellectual beginnings the two streams of anti-bourgeois agitation naturally came to different views of social action. The political writers—Marxists, Proudhonians, Saint-Simonians, Fourierists—concerned themselves with a social response to bourgeois rule which was conceived as a power counterthrust to power. These men applauded the material benefits made possible by bourgeois economic enterprise, but demanded an end to the new forms of injustice inaugurated by it. The literary rebels, on the other hand, were interested in the rights of the few. Their claims were made in the name of obeisance to taste, beauty, and the sovereignty of special intelligence and creative power. They did not, as we shall see, criticize the bourgeoisie so much for its heartlessness as for its vulgarity and the insignificance of its life aims. From such a "spiritual" point of view it often appeared to literary men that the only important difference between the bourgeoisie and the proletariat was the capacity of the first to exploit the second. Aside from this the two seemed one in their common devotion to material gratifications. In other words, the literary rebels were individualistic without being democratic, just as they tended to be esoteric and pessimistic; socialists and reformists, of course, tended to be progressive, scientific, and optimistic. Seeing themselves as a small, embattled company of select spirits in the midst of a massive onslaught of materialistic grasping, the literary men became self-conscious, easily threatened, and almost unappeasable in their intellectual fastidiousness. But it would be wrong to say that they had no view of the social order or the proper society. They did. It was that of a hierarchical world resting on the discipline established by reverence to intelligence and to the spiritual poise and aesthetic and moral superiority of a new aristocracy—themselves.

NOTES TO CHAPTER VI

1. Benedetto Croce, *La Borghesia* (Bari: Gino La Terza, 1945), pp. 7-9.

2. Karl Marx, *Capital* (New York: Modern Library), p. 25; Karl Marx, *The German Ideology* (New York: International Publishers, 1939), p. 15.

3. Karl Marx, *The Eighteenth Brumaire of Louis Bonaparte* (Chicago: Charles H. Kerr & Co., 1913), p. 53.

4. Harold Rosenberg, "The Proletarian Pathos," *The Kenyon Review,* Autumn, 1949, p. 619.

5. Nicolas Lenin, *What Is to Be Done?* (London: Martin Lawrence), Chapter II.

6. Karl Marx & Frederic Engels, *Selected Correspondence* (New York: International Publishers, 1934), p. 416.

7. *Grand dictionnaire universel du XIXe siècle* (17 vols.; Paris: 1867), **II**, 1124.

8. Karl Marx, *The Communist Manifesto,* Samuel H. Beer, ed. (New York: Appleton-Century-Crofts, Inc., 1955), Part I.

9. *Grand dictionnaire,* p. 1121.

10. *Ibid.,* p. 1124.

11. Louis Blanc, *op. cit.,* p. 100.

12. Jacques Barzun, *Romanticism and the Modern Ego* (New York: Harcourt, Brace & Co., 1944), pp. 213 f.

13. Arthur O. Lovejoy, "On the Discrimination of Romanticisms," *P.M.I.A.,* **XXXIX** (1924), 229.

14. The term is used by Bertrand Russell in "Byron and the Modern World," *Journal of the History of Ideas,* **I**, No. 1, 25.

15. The term is used by Helene Frejlich in *Flaubert d'après sa correspondance* (Paris: Société française d'éditions littéraires et techniques, 1933), p. 269.

CHAPTER VII

THE IDEOLOGICAL
SIGNIFICANCE OF
BOHEMIAN LIFE

THE NEW LITERARY IDEALS and the struggling, searching, voluble young men who were their natural protagonists joined together in Paris to make of intellectual discontent a cultural spectacle. They created *la vie de bohème* as a means of intruding into daily reality their willful and unpredictable energies, their thrust for novelty, and their colorful contempt for the established spiritual order. The language of Bohemia, said Henri de Mürger (who was to make his reputation as the chief chronicler of the garret) was a paradise to experimentalists and a hell to classicists. And Alexandre Dumas, when he felt like posing as a Bohemian, at once assumed the idiom of self-dramatized and shimmering sensitivity and the air of unstable, pulsing intellectual excitement; "a brush in one hand, a pen in the other, laughing, crying, scribbling." [1] Balzac, on the other hand, in *A Prince of Bohemia,* saw Bohemian glamor and even Bohemian fun as the symbol of enforced failure, the spectacle of young intellectuals who had turned to iconoclasm and exhibitionism, because of their frustration before what he called the "gerontocracy" of the Restoration and Orleanist periods. If the Tsar would buy Bohemia and set it down in Odessa, Odessa would be Paris within a year. There were, he said, writers, administrators, soldiers, artists, and diplomats in Bohemia "quite capable of overturning Russia's designs, if they but felt the power of France at their backs." [2]

Most writers who succeed in their work are, in the strict sense, unsatisfactory Bohemians. True Bohemian sectarianism is usually carried on by people of excitable imaginations and modest talent, a combination which disables them for an ordinary existence and forces them, as consolation, to a life of dedicated unconventionality. For the really talented, as Balzac suggests, Bohemia is a stimulating interlude until the chance for real work arrives. Yet, Balzac knew that within Bohemia, as generally within modern literary life, there was a struggle between the most passionate ambition and the fear that success would mean only the kiss of death to freedom and integrity. As he put it in his curious piece of speculation about Paris and Odessa, even if Russia were thrown open to the intellectual colonization of young Parisians they might not choose to leave "the asphalt of the boulevards behind them." [3] The point is that, although Bohemia has never been, as such, the house of the intellect, the spirit of intellectual vagrancy which it represents has considerable ideological significance and an affectionately legendary place in the world of artists and writers. Every literary generation since the nineteenth century has had its Bohemian moment, and the inheritance shows in some detail of personal display, in the occasions of spiritual revelry and comradeship observed in the academy, the studio, and the newspaperman's saloon, and in the paraphernalia and voluntary stigmata of Latin Quarters everywhere. The reason is that Bohemia embodies as a social fixture the burning and doomed enthusiasm for the life of the spirit, the daily battle against the powers of the modern world. As the founders of this tradition, the Parisian Bohemians created a fellowship which a young artist or writer could become a part of, invented the basic Bohemian manner, and named it appropriately with a variant of the French word for gypsy. For the Bohemian image has always been an intellectually uplifted version of the gypsy image as a community of chosen outcasts, claiming the spontaneous gift of creativity and willing to undergo great penalties to preserve their peculiar freedoms. By its very nature Bohemia was too impersonal, unbusinesslike, and lacking in unified goals to become an organized utopia in the sense of a Brook Farm or a religious community. But it did represent the intention to translate into daily experience the romantic code of existence for the sake of beauty, creative work, and the free individual who was the servant and, if necessary, the victim of such values. In other words, it created the sociological props for the literary existence as a "subculture," as a public way of life.

One of the recurrent features of a period calling into question established social principle seems to be to drive young people into unexpected forms of defiance and unrest.

The French Revolution, for example, had, as one of its aftermaths, the appearance of youthful gangs and coteries dedicated to the cultivation of special passions and adventures. Some, like the Unbelievables (*Incroyables*) of the Thermidorian reaction, were aristocratic and monarchist and had as their purpose the terrorizing of their radical counterparts of the Jacobin Club. Their clothing identification (always a concomitant of youth groups) was expensive and precise—abundant lace, high cravat, tight trousers, a short velvet waistcoat with eighteen mother-of-pearl buttons, and artificial beauty marks. Their hair was cut short in the back and hung over the face in free locks. The style was a piece of macabre taunting called *à la victime* because it imitated the appearance of a person about to be placed under the guillotine. Others, like the *Bousingots* (one translation is the "Hell-raisers") of the Restoration Period, were apparently recruited from among middle-class discontents and held radical-sounding, erratic political ideas which somehow were never followed by practical action. According to Balzac they could be recognized by their off-center cravats, greasy coats, long beards, and dirty finger nails.[4] The Bohemians of the 1830's and 1840's were young, actually and ideologically; they claimed that youth itself was the collective expression of genius. It is exaggerating very little to say that Bohemians hoped to be seen as a band of intellectual raiders and freebooters, who routed convention everywhere and kept all contented souls in a state of dazzled alarm. In this, if we believe Mrs. Trollope, they succeeded only too well. In 1836, she wrote that, "Young France," (one of the Bohemian tags) had become a cabalistic figure of speech "by which everybody seems to be expected to understand something great, terrible, volcanic and sublime."[5] In all accounts of the Bohemia of the Orleanist years, the first impressions have always to do with its ingenious techniques of social outrage. When Thackeray first came on the Paris Bohemia, he was astonished enough to make a careful record of their appearance—their ringlets, straight locks, toupees, English, Greek and Spanish nets, and the variety of their beards and jackets.[6] The painter Pelletier went on walks accompanied by a pet jackal. De Nerval took a lobster on a leash through the Tuilleries gardens; "It does not bark," he said, "and knows the secrets of the deep." Théophile Gautier's red waistcoat staggered the bourgeois at the premiere of *Hernani,* though by Bohemian standards such apparel was in no way extraordinary. In the recollection of Hugo's wife, the Hugoiste claque at this most storied of first nights also wore Spanish cloaks, Robespierre waistcoats, and Henry III caps.[7] *

---

* Dumas, Balzac, de Vigny, Sainte-Beuve, Mérimée, and Nodier were all present at *Hernani*'s opening. Stendhal was also there, though he was not friendly toward Hugo or his group. Hugo's band from the Latin Quarter was of about four hundred. The rioting began almost with the first line. Jeering throughout the performance from his box was Scribe, the most successful (and the wealthiest) of the conventional dramatists. J. B. Priestley, *Literature and Western Man* (New York: Harper & Brothers, 1960), pp. 164-165.

Obviously prankish as these things were, there stood behind them the effort to give manner and presence to the aristocratic credo of the new intelligentsia. However, as was pointed out in an earlier chapter, this credo did not represent a continuation or revival of the Old Regime's learned courtliness. On the contrary, at least in the Bohemian case, the chosen gained a sense of their condition, either from the reverse pride of the citizen of an outcast world or from an identification with the glamorous aggression and egotism of the outlaw. For, in the sense that romanticism is a glorification of "predatory efficiency" (the basis, according to Thorstein Veblen, of barbaric elites),[8] Bohemian imagination was, above all, romantic, that is to say, filled with bandits, pirates, robber barons, and other such heroes who were at the same time aristocratic and primitive, splendid and threatening. It is not surprising, therefore, that in their farewell notes to the world the young Parisian suicides of Mrs. Trollope's day would speak of yearning for a greatness that "should cost neither labor nor care" and express "profound contempt for those who are satisfied to live by the sweat of their brow."[9]

Of course, the aesthete's war was bound to be a war of the imagination—a member of Gautier's circle wrote that, while Saint-Simonians and Fourierists attacked the bourgeoisie at the political and economic level, the artistic faction had as its weapons only "the brush, the lyre, and the chisel."[10] And perhaps for that reason, it was waged with a degree of psychological aggression which reached near-cultist proportions. Examining the dramatists of the 1830's, Mrs. Trollope was taken aback by their infatuation with vice, poison, rape, murder, and blasphemy. Gautier himself spoke of the "carrion novels" written by his contemporaries. "Black humor" and talking "graveyard stuff" (*parler cadavre*) became essential to the jargon of the Bohemians.[11] The painters appeared to Châteaubriand to have, in addition to their alarming mustaches, heads full of deluges, seas, rivers, forests, cataracts, tempests, slaughters, and tortures.

Their aim, he said, was to form a separate species between the ape and the satyr.[12] The accuracy of this reading of the artist's inner thoughts as a forecast of the character of the art itself is attested by the death, massacre, and battle scenes which became the staple of so much romantic painting.*

Just as Bohemians dreamed of themselves as the protagonists of picturesque violence, so were their anecdotes and stunts symbolic acts of terror on society. Skeletons provided "atmosphere" for many garrets and were sometimes used for such primeval apocalyptic gestures as the famous attempts by Borel, Gautier, and de Nerval to quaff sea water out of a human skull. Borel called his quarters "The Tartar War Camp," and de Nerval pitched a nomad's tent in the middle of his apartment. The *Bousingots* were said to eat wild boar ("not digestible, but Gothic") and to hang their walls with tomahawks and "poisoned" daggers. The constitution of one student band, the *Badouillards,* required its members to be initiated at a nightlong vigil, during which they guarded arms in the medieval fashion to show courage in fighting and proficiency in fencing and boxing. They took an oath of vengeance on the bourgeoisie, and had to display a repertory of obscene songs suitable for disturbing the peace.[13]

The following (a poem in prose translation), by Théophile Dondey,† is a typical document of the period.

---

* Among the titles of paintings noted down by Thackeray at an exhibit in the 1830's are the following: "The Massacre at Scio," "Medea Going to Murder Her Children," "Hecuba Going to Be Sacrificed," "The Grand Dauphiness Dying," "Zenobia Found Dead," "The Death of Caesar," "The Death of Hector," "The Massacre of St. Bartholomew," "Young Clovis Found Dead," "Cain after the Death of Abel," "Death of Philip of Austria," "Death of Queen Elizabeth," "Death of Lucretia," "Death of Hymetto," "Death of Adelaide of Cominges." Thackeray, *op. cit.,* pp. 67-68.

† In keeping with the romantic attachment to the Scottish highlands, and the glamorous wildness of their nature and customs, Théophile Dondey changed his name to Philotée O'Neddy.

In the center of the room, round a blazing punch bowl whose prysmatic flames resemble a steamy lake, and whose size is the equal of the expanses of Hell, sit twenty young men, artists to the core, pipes puffing, sardonic of eye, their heads adorned with the Liberty Cap; the bearded Young France ready for the orgy. . . . In the morning these Fate-touched Young Men will revel in a river of wrathful madness, will grasp their daggers, pledge themselves to rip open the bellies of the money-counters, and swear to devote their lives to waging war against these barren times. . . .[14]

What Dondey offers us here is a short catalogue of Bohemian romantic hatreds and devotions: the chosen Young Man, beautiful, satanic, savage and sensitive; the witchcraft (and the burden) of genius; the soul-deprived world, languishing under the sterile tyranny of the merchant; the duty of the creative outcast to be reckless and free; the Avenging Angel of Art who will finally plunge the knife into the heart of bourgeois society—that is, its stomach.

The dadaistic clowning and esoteric jokes which have always been hallmarks of Bohemia also flourished among these originals. In their stories women died laughing, while lovers tickled their feet. Their chapter headings were written in English, Latin, Provençal, and Spanish. Their books had titles like *On the Incommodiousness of Commodes* or *On the Effect of the Tales of Fishes upon the Undulations of the Sea*. The preface to a book by Dondey read:

> Ah
> Eh he
> He! hi! hi!
> Oh
> Hu! Hu! Hu!
> Profession of faith of the author.[15]

Yet all of this provocative tomfoolery was designed to furnish comic relief for a profound feeling of frustration and abhorrence. If Théophile Dondey's "profession of faith" was a stammering of gibberish it was only because, as he wrote Borel,

"Like you, I despise society. . . and especially its excrescence, the social order." [16]

One cause of cynicism was political bewilderment. Gautier complained that his "best enemies" advised him to be red one day and white the next (and out of boredom he concluded that "poets, dreamers, and musicians had no business trying to be good citizens").[17] Early in Mürger's *Vie de Bohème,* Rodolphe, the young artist, instructs the *concierge* in charge of his garret to awaken him every morning by announcing the day of the week, the day of the month, the quarter of the moon, and the form of the government.[18] After two generations of revolution, war, propaganda, and countless panaceas, there were those who could only respond with exhaustion, hilarity, and contempt, or seek the respite of new forms of imagination. Yet it was precisely political confusion that permitted Bohemian life to exist. For however the bourgeoisie might defile the life of the spirit, it lacked the ideological bone structure capable of placing all of society under the pale of one jealous and inflexible order. Bohemia, for its part, despite all of the burning bitterness of its anti-social feeling, was, almost by definition, politically powerless. What it caused to flourish instead was, in Dondey's words, the "arsenal of the soul," the pursuit of purely ideal engagements. Of these the most typical and the most influential historically was the religion of beauty, *l'art pour l'art,* a kingdom whose integrity was free from the secular world, whose tasks arose only out of the individual's own creativity and which, therefore, permitted the gratification of the romantic need to be at the same time significant and self-centered.

Art for art's sake was a saving vision. It was also a sectarian devotion exhibiting and accepting the martyrdom of philistine incomprehension, or as Châteaubriand called it, "the pageant of the bleeding heart." [19] What this meant to a generation without religious faith and incapable of social optimism may be seen in the theatrically sincere notes of office workers, law clerks, and minor *fonctionnaires* collected by the literary historian

René Maigron, in which obscure young men pay the symbolic homage of life and death to the romantic dream of redeeming beauty. One, written by a "future littérateur" in 1836, says:

> I shall open my breast to the great wind of Art and my quivering heart will ecstatically exult while my ship, upon the wind of beauty will joyfully sail over the purple sea. Far, far and even farther, believe not in the abyss. Fly my beautiful vessel, far from the hated shore. Higher and always higher. We shall lull sweetly along, over the misty expanses, toward the enchanted dream.[20]

Another reads:

> Heroes die smiling in the flames, and like them, I go smiling to the funeral pyre. Divine Art, I carry you in my soul. Let me be worthy of you.[21]

For men so precious, so exacting, and so vulnerable, death appeared, understandably, as the only harbor open to lonely sensibility. Their books had titles like *Nécropolis, Philosophie du désespoir, Entre la vie et la mort, Mémoires d'un suicide,* and *L'Amour de la mort.* According to Sainte-Beuve the ideal of the romantic generation was to be a great poet and to die. "Never was death more loved than then," said Maxime DuCamp speaking of the romantic years and the sensuous necrophilia of writers for whom death had "the delicate aroma of flowers or perfume" bears him out.[22]

There were, in fact, some semi-serious efforts to formalize the suicidal ideal, such as *The Suicide Club* (originally called the Fed-ups Club) organized at the Sorbonne in 1846. *The Suicide Club* recruited its members between the ages of eighteen and thirty. It pledged them to show the bourgeoisie that nothing could be nobler than self-destruction. It excluded those wishing to end their lives because of disappointment in love, financial difficulties, or incurable disease. And it prohibited all suicide methods likely to cause disfiguration.[23] Romanticism, which united art and life, art and self, and death and self, was also bound to unite death and art. It is, therefore, perfectly fitting

that the poet Théophile Dondey should choose the surroundings of grand opera as the ideal setting for his final moment.

> I would sit alone in a quiet box, and when the violins, the oboes, and
> the musical throats rise like sonorous arches before the admiring
> heart. I shall swallow a handful of some bliss-bringing opiate. . .
> as the chaste-sensuous music pours out its homage to my beautiful
> death.[24]

After the suicides of the young dramatists Escousse and Le-
bras, there was talk in the newspapers of self-killing as "the
devouring plague of the times," and speeches were made in the
Chamber of Deputies blaming the excesses of literary excitement.[25] Still, one must not expect death as an ideal to be followed by death in fact. Goethe survived *The Sorrows of Young
Werther* and Rousseau *La Nouvelle Héloïse*. Even de Senancour did not listen to his own suicidal advocacies in *Obermann,*
though there would seem to be no retreat from them. *The
Suicide Club* was, of course, an elaborately outrageous joke
aimed chiefly at a *succès de scandale;* only one suicide among
its members was actually reported. But intellectually it was a
testimony to death as "the only airtight Bohemia." [26] It warned
against disfiguration so as to protect aesthetic pride to the last.
And it taught that, just as ordinary contentment made life
void and vulgar, commonplace forms of suffering, like money
troubles, heartbreaks and ill health, rendered death spiritually
meaningless.

The Suicide Club and other necrophilic displays of Bohemia
were, of course, linked to the fatuously masochistic side of romanticism. But they remind us all the same of de Lamennais'
observation that self-killing was essentially an act of self-wor-
ship and, as such, one of the chief signs of modern decay. In
this respect, de Lamennais merely anticipated the theories of
the classical sociologists. Compare, for example, de Lamennais' analysis with that of Émile Durkheim in the latter's famous
study, *Suicide*. According to de Lamennais:

One can flatter pride with vain promises of independence, but one cannot cure the wound of the heart. As man moves away from order, anguish presses around him. He is the king of his own misery, a degraded sovereign in revolt against himself, without duties and without bonds, without society. Alone in the midst of the universe, he runs rather than seeks to run away into nothingness.[27]

De Lamennais is solemn and ironic; Durkheim is factual and brief. But their arguments are essentially the same. Durkheim writes:

Therefore, the educated man who kills himself, does not kill himself because he is educated but because the religious society of which he is a part has lost its cohesion.[28]

This statement, however, is only part of Durkheim's theory of suicide as a product of the moral watering-down of institutions of modern society. He comes closer to the relationship between suicidal ideas and the ailments of the modern *literati* when he points out that it was precisely the utopian intensity of their aesthetic and intellectual dreams that led to bitterness and demoralization. It should not be thought, of course, that, as a philosophical argument, individualistic suicide was an invention of the nineteenth century. Montesquieu attacked European legislation on suicide as too severe; for, why, he asked, should a man who is poor, unhappy, or scorned by his fellows be compelled to remain within society? [29] The psychologist and philosopher Baron Holbach argued simply that "the pact that binds man to society . . . is conditional and reciprocal, and a society which cannot bring well-being to us loses all rights upon us." [30] In Montesquieu there is a dismissal of the old odium against suicide which saw in it always a defiance of man's obligation to social membership regardless of subjective sufferings. Holbach speaks for the view of the Enlightenment that society was only a contract among individuals for the benefit of individuals, and thus turns suicide into a kind of civil right. But it is only with Durkheim's description of *suicide égoïste* that we step into the atmosphere of modern literary motivations.

Social man necessarily presupposes a society which he expresses and serves. If it dissolves, if we no longer feel its existence and action about and above us. . . all that remains is an artificial combination of illusory images and phantasmagoria vanishing at the least reflection: that is, nothing that can be a goal for our action.[31]

For de Nerval, the potency of a released imagination had swept the mind of his contemporaries toward "love" and "poetry," and away from the crowd and its greed. However, George Sand looking at the same state of mind, saw it as the spectacle of the anguish and fatigue created by a self-centered intellectual ambition "grown and stretched beyond measure." Durkheim, in speaking of "vanishing phantasmagorias" and "the artificial combination of illusory images," suggests that the *tour d'ivoire* was also a *tour de force* which literary self-will could not in the end sustain. Rationalism had seen the emancipation of man from faith as a victory. The romantics may also have seen faith as defenseless before the analytical mind. But for them the consequence was self-defeat. In George Sand's novel *Lélia,* as the young poet nears suicide, he seems to voice the Durkheimian theory in the form of a literary outcry.

I know. . . there is nothing true in man's dreams, and that once truth is unveiled, there is nothing for man but the endurance of anxiety, the resolve to live with despair. And when I said that man can be gratified through his own powers I lied to others and to myself; for he who arrives at the possession of useless powers, to the exercise of energies without worth and goals, is nothing but a vigorous fool. . . .[32]

NOTES TO CHAPTER VII

1. Cited in *Grand Dictionnaire,* **II**, 866.
2. Honoré de Balzac, *La Comédie humaine,* **XII**, 79-80.
3. *Ibid.,* p. 80.
4. Théophile Lavallée, *Histoire de Paris* (Paris: J. Hetzel, 1852), p. 421.

5. Trollope, *op. cit.*, pp. 58-59.

6. Thackeray, *op. cit.*, pp. 58-59.

7. Williams, *op. cit.*, pp. 29-30; Starkie, *op. cit.*, pp. 29, 83, 91; J. B. Priestley, *Literature and Western Man* (New York: Harper & Brothers, 1960), p. 171.

8. Thorstein Veblen, *The Theory of the Leisure Class* (New York: Modern Library, 1934), pp. 18 f.

9. Trollope, *op. cit.*, p. 197.

10. Gautier, *op. cit.*, p. 85.

11. Starkie, *op. cit.*, pp. 56, 94, 112.

12. In Irving Babbitt, *Rousseau and Romanticism* (New York: Meridian Books, 1955), p. 61.

13. Williams, *op. cit.*, p. 29; Starkie, *op. cit.*, pp. 84, 86, 89.

14. Williams, *op. cit.*, pp. 150-151; Starkie, *op. cit.*, p. 92. Williams and Starkie quote different portions of this poem. I have given a reconstruction in free translation of both portions.

15. Cited in Starkie, *op. cit.*, p. 197.

16. Cited in Louis Maigron, *Le Romantisme et les moeurs* (Paris: Honoré Champion, 1910), p. 360.

17. In *ibid.*, p. 357.

18. Mürger, *op. cit.*, p. 28.

19. Wellek, *op. cit.*, **II**, p. 238.

20. Cited in Maigron, *op. cit.*, p. 81.

21. Cited in *ibid.*, p. 79.

22. Starkie, *op. cit.*, p. 60.

23. Maigron, *op. cit.*, pp. 341-342.

24. Cited in Maigron, *op. cit.*, p. 329.

25. Trollope, *op. cit.*, p. 197.

26. The expression is Leslie Fiedler's. *An End to Innocence* (Boston: Beacon Press, 1952), p. 183.

27. De Lamennais, *op. cit.*, Part **I**, p. 151.

28. Émile Durkheim, *Suicide* (Glencoe, Illinois: The Free Press, 1951), p. 169.

29. De Montesquieu, *Oeuvres complètes,* Edouard Laboulaye, editor (7 vols.; Paris: Barnier Frères, 1875), **I**, 254-257.

30. Baron Holbach (M. Mirabaud, pseudonym) *Système de la nature* (2 vols.; London, 1771), **I**, 329 f.

31. Durkheim, *op. cit.*, p. 213.

32. George Sand, *Lélia* (Paris: Garnier Frères, 1960), p. 288.

Part 2

Three Literary Critics of Bourgeois Society: Stendhal, Flaubert, and Baudelaire

CHAPTER VIII

BOURGEOIS ENTERPRISE
AND MODERN LIFE:
CULTURAL DEVALUATION AND
THE RISING MARKET

IF WE GATHER the conclusions of the previous chapters, the social and intellectual conditions of French literature in the nineteenth century appear as follows: a "sponsor" class no longer existed, writers no longer played their part on a stage of cultural continuity and, as in the case of competing ideologies and economic interests, literature had become subject to the modern market place. Therefore, by necessity (as well as by wish), the writer was left to stand before a depersonalized audience. This had at least two consequences. One was anxiety and suspicion. The other was heroic illusion. Writers found it difficult to endure their dependence on a disembodied reader and were tortured by the problem of gaining public approval for the personal canons of their work. The result was defiance, certain forms of intimate intellectual sectarianism, and self-assertion through martyrdom, of which suicide was, perhaps, the prototype ideal. But, as in the optical illusion that turns the picture of a cube into a box when shifted under the light, the writer could look on a faceless society as a large, lethargic organism that could be galvanized into an admiring collective being by a single, imperial personality. The vast, distant menace of the crowd became transformed into the horizon across which coursed the proverbial meteoric career. Finally, there was the great issue of intellectual morality and imagination, the refusal of the modern writer to acknowledge the terms of human life created and demanded by the bourgeoisie. This impasse, oddly enough, was caused by two forms of individualism arising out of the same historical situation. The bourgeoisie had created a society of individualized goals and, in that sense, made possible and even invited literary individualism. But while bourgeois individualism had economic and political targets and looked on the world as something concretely to be measured, governed, and used, literary individualism was wholly centered on the person as an intellectual and imaginative reality. The literary individualist, therefore, was bound to find the mundane boundaries of bourgeois effort and ambition intolerable.

Some of the early responses to the middle class as a cultural factor were friendly and optimistic. It was greeted as a vehicle of progress, capable of objective decisions and free of the weight of custom and tradition. The following, for example, are Voltaire's impressions of English merchants:

Enter the London stock exchange, that more respectable place than many a court; you will see the deputies of all nations gathered there for the service of mankind. There the Jew, the Mohammedan, and the Christian deal together as if they were of the same religion, and apply the name of infidel only to those who go bankrupt; there the Presbyterian trusts the Anabaptist, and the Anglican accepts the Quaker promise. On leaving these peaceful and free assemblies, some go to the synagogue, others go to drink; one goes to have himself baptized in the name of the Father, through the Son to the Holy Ghost; another has his son's foreskin cut off and Hebrew words mumbled over him which he does not understand; others go to their church to await the inspiration of God with their hats on their heads; and all are content.[1]

The point here, clearly is not that religious tolerance is good for business (though one could infer from what Voltaire says that the pure business mind will not let religion stand in the way of gain). Religion, in fact, is regarded as an idiosyncratic psychological vestige of small significance. The important thing is that, like other men of the Enlightenment, Voltaire took it for granted that the rational self-interest of individuals would flow into a common tide of social benefits. The merchants, by putting their market transactions above the emotional and ceremonial traditions of their separate religious groups, were really acting in the service of humanity.

Marx too, as we know, had great admiration for the "objective" relations created by the bourgeoisie through its destruction of the traditional basis of cultural and psychological life. For him, however, the bourgeoisie was unable to conquer the provincialism of class interests; it could not match ideologically the consequences of its own social and technological revolution. The working class, on the other hand, and particularly its "advanced section" (the Communist Party), represented the further intellectual transformation which would permit men not only to understand the character of modern society generally but to look over the horizon into "the line of march" of the future.[2]*

Marxism was part of a century of great intellectual agitation and intellectual hope. From radicals to conservatives, from dreamers to realists, one finds everywhere the same sense of urgency and challenge before new and disturbing social realities, and the same determination to discover the meaning of those realities for the modern world. The large theories and all-embracing programs of social reconstruction and reform during this period were, no doubt, an expression of intellectual conceit

---

* A subsidiary type, straddling between bourgeois rationalism and socialist rationalism, may be found in the Saint-Simonian movement, which proposed a partnership of financiers, technologists, and ideologists for the scientific contrivance of a new human community.

—of the belief that only the thinker could shoulder the burden of society's troubles. Still, even the most utopian of such programs was intended to link the intellectual man to the common man.

The protagonists of literary rebelliousness, on the other hand, were often unmoved by social causes and were utopian only in very private ways. Neither were they by design social thinkers nor, in the sociologist's sense, objective. When they addressed themselves to social conditions they did so in the form of warnings, comments, and attacks. They had what social scientists regard as the normal drawbacks of the literary person as a social observer. One should note in this respect that early sociological writing neglected realms of social experience which, to the literary mind, appeared as the really essential facts of modern life. For example, what was the relation between the new social circumstances and personal values? What was the moral and psychological style of the new order? What was the new repertory of human aspirations, the new image of social rewards? Was there a change in the fabric of emotional relationships among men, or between men and their work? It is only ironical that some social scientists who today struggle to understand the link between public developments and the person's inner sense might well find themselves in closer fellowship with the work of literary commentators than with the more panoramic minds officially responsible for the founding of their profession.

Of these free-lance observers three have been chosen— Stendhal (Henri Beyle), Gustave Flaubert, and Charles Baudelaire—as much for their historical sensitivity as for their literary eminence. None of them could be called "responsible," if by this we mean that they intended their work as a contribution to the social welfare. They were, on the contrary, disillusioned almost beforehand, meticulously skeptical, and certainly unmoved by anything resembling a "social problem" in the usual sense. They regarded the society around them as a mixture of triviality and barbarism and, unlike social theorists and reformers, they took pride in their isolation from it. Only this isolation, they felt, made it possible for them to endure and to observe it.

The three men were different in their tempers and their skills. Baudelaire lived at the top of his subjective sufferings, discussing social questions in passionate religious allegory and battling between self-pity and a regal sense of spiritual elegance. Flaubert was a psychological realist who never quite overcame the romantic longing and disillusionment of his time. Stendhal moved with an unshakable nonchalance which allowed him to produce clinically detached annotations on Orleanist society. But they all had remarkably similar cultural and intellectual concerns, and they blamed the modern distress on the same social and historical events—the rule of the businessman, the democratization of experience, and the impact of technology and business on the psychological organization of life.

Generally speaking, the city represents the most influential collection of values in the contemporary world and we might begin by considering the attitude of the three writers toward this major fact. Very simply they were all city-lovers and province-haters. Baudelaire despised the countryside, refusing to believe that trees had once been worshiped as gods, and professing to be upset by the sight of running water.[3] At first this appears as a paradox inasmuch as the market society, against which all three raged for a lifetime, was pre-eminently an urban phenomenon. But the question must be understood on a different symbolic level. The point of Baudelaire's jokes and taunts was directed at the province as the anti-type of the intellectual life. The sin of the province was not its economic inferiority or physical modesty (none of these writers are big-city snobs in the ordinary materialistic sense) but the spiritual torpor which made it "the breeding ground of blockheads, the most stupid of milieus, the most productive of absurdities, the most abundant in intolerant imbeciles."[4] Stendhal, on the other hand, was concerned with the human rather than with the cultural lag. The province had been his own point of entry into the world ("where I learned to know men"), and had given him his first lesson in wariness and cynicism. These touchstones, sluggishness and philistinism, reappear in Flaubert's castigations* of the middle class. To the moral and cultural picture, however, he adds what might be called the sociological or, at any rate, the occupational elements. Life in the provinces, he says, was ruled by the fact that "there the common people are incessantly engaged in little employments the very nature of which distort their ideas." [5]

It is Stendhal who, in the midst of these asperities, names things with a familiar name. The "lowness," the "meanness," and the "horror" which he says he had known in his native city of Grenoble were the lowness, meanness, and horror of the middle class,[6] the natural product of its stagnant smugness and its monotonous greed. The province was bourgeois. In fact, by virtue of its very isolation, the province was able to expose the nuggets of the bourgeois soul with an essential clarity and perfection. This at once explains the meaning of Flaubert's reference to the provincial prevalence of "little employments." Dedication to spiritually vacant tasks (which is what he means by "little employments") was one of the caste marks of the bourgeoisie. Anyone who acquired a routine social obligation or worked at a profession received from Flaubert either casual scorn or mocking sorrow. When his friend Ernest Chevalier became a lawyer and later married, Flaubert at once predicted that, having chosen to uphold property and family, he was bound to end up as a reactionary magistrate and a cuckold and that, "thus spending his life between his wife and children and the idiocy of his job," he would have happily found within him-

---

* Flaubert's general broadside at the province as "the home of imbecility, the most stupid society, the most productive of absurdities, the most abundant in intolerant fools," is clearly borrowed from or by Baudelaire.

self all the qualities of the average man.[7] This contempt for the "job," for the discharge of a habitual task, was pushed to a fine dramatic extreme by Baudelaire when he said that there were only three men worthy of respect—the priest, the warrior, and the poet—and that the rest of mankind was "born for the stable, that is to say, to practice what they call professions." [8] What is inherent in all of these strictures is that, for the disaffected literary man, the common denominator of the bourgeois man was the fact of his social resourcefulness. Stendhal saw him as "meticulous in advancing his own little schemes," and Flaubert saw him as "plodding and avaricious" (Stendhal's reaction to this was "to weep and vomit at the same time," and Flaubert's "almost the rage of hydrophobia").[9] But, whatever his vices, the bourgeois was productive. If his mind did not understand art neither did it understand disillusionment. "One must establish oneself. . . . one must be useful. . . . man is born to work." This was, according to Flaubert, the personal and social credo of the bourgeois.[10] Its passwords were productiveness and utility, which was just why he ought to be denied and castigated. Baudelaire was being perfectly straightforward when he said, "to be a useful person has always appeared to me to be something particularly horrible." [11]

At first glance these words read like a curiously undignified pronouncement, an unpleasant *enfant terrible* joke. They seem unnecessarily, even absurdly, offensive. But it is not difficult to understand the uneasiness of a writer before men who concern themselves only with the avenues of power. Art has never been a skill indispensable to the conduct of social life and this precariousness makes its practitioners sensitive as, in fact, it makes them vulnerable. Still, such a peculiar mixture of bitterness and flippancy in scorning the entire principle of social utility seems a little surprising. To explain it, one is forced into nothing less than a complete examination of what Baudelaire (and Stendhal and Flaubert) thought of the nature of culture, of the nature of man, of the purpose of life, and the role of the creative person.

Like many men of their time these three writers were alarmed by the dangers which they saw in the domination of life by modern industry, technology, and commercial aggressiveness. All three felt that modern economic enterprise endangered the natural balance of cultural existence and the spontaneous psychological needs of men—perhaps even distracted them from a rational apprehension of life's true tasks and problems. Let us explore these broad accusations.

A preoccupation with the economic dispossession and uprootedness caused by industrialization, the oppressiveness of early machinery and work methods, the enslavement of children, the rise of large-scale prostitution, the poorhouse, the infested makeshift slums—all of these are familiar features of nineteenth-century social literature. Protests, theories, and relief schemes came from all sides: from the Proudhonians, the Catholic "Pauperists," Louis Blanc and his "national workshops" movement, the Saint-Simonians (who coined such staple terminology of the class struggle as "exploitation," "solidarity," "wage-earner," "capitalist," and "proletarian"), and later, of course, the Marxian socialists. Even someone like Stendhal, who lacked all democratic sentiment and was not particularly sensitive to human suffering, seems to have been, if not disturbed, at least bothered by French industrial conditions and once wondered whether a mere account of what he had witnessed at the Nivernais forges in Northern France might not be sufficient to indict him as a "Jacobin." [12]

However, Stendhal's concern with modern productive methods was directed to more subjective matters than "exploitation" or "wage slavery." What really worried him was the impact of the new economic conditions on man's capacity to respond freely to the varied stimulation of life. While visiting England he had observed Birmingham workers bending over their tasks "with ferocious obstinacy," all human ease and feeling drained out of them by the pressure of their jobs. He concluded from this and other impressions that in all "advanced" nations people, both professionals and workers, would become irrationally "victimized by labor." (In England, according to him, judges and manual toilers attacked their jobs with the same grim determination.) This would stunt their discernment of the true essentials of human behavior, or, as he put it, "subtleties in ideas or events," and destroy the sensuous and aesthetic response to life which had been the traditional basis of happiness for all classes.[13]

Flaubert, like Stendhal, witnessed only the early stages of industrialization. But he, too, feared it for its mind-dwarfing pressures and numbing invasion of sense-life ("what din has industry brought into the world. What a noisy thing the machine is!") and for the spawning of countless "idiotic occupations" leading to "mass stupidity."[14] According to Baudelaire, this "cruel, implacable regularity" of industry could be traced to the spiritual source of the system itself, the modern business house.[15] There was for Baudelaire no greater menace to human integrity than money and machines, and the combination of barren rationalism and materialistic craving which they nourished.

Mechanization will have so Americanized us, Progress will have so well atrophied us, our entire spiritual part, that nothing among the sanguinary, sacrilegious or unnatural dreams of the modern utopians will be able to be compared with their positive results.[16]

The use of words like "sanguinary," "sacrilegious," and "unnatural" reveals, not unwittingly, the depths of hatred and fear with which Baudelaire and others looked on the emerging forces of nineteenth-century life—equality, science, technology, and the demands for material well-being. When the painter Delacroix visited the International Exposition of 1834 in Paris he left greatly disturbed after seeing a machine which, by turning a crank, made flowers bloom out of an artificial branch. Clearly his uneasiness was caused by the reproduction, mechanically and at will, of a "mysterious" natural event. Baudelaire saw this process taking place on a scale which encompassed all of society and all of life. The regularization of modern experience through technology was "the negation of God by the steam engine," a denial of the divine in men's lives. Only by living life as a problem and predicament, the meaning of which was always to be partially hidden, could society attain the moral tension and spiritual awareness needed for a deep and vital sense of purpose. The cult of progress based on a principle of mechanical inevitability contained no self-imposed challenges, no exertion of the inner person, and could, at best, deliver nothing more than the fodder of materialistic indulgence. He called it, for that reason, "the cult of the lazy and the idiotic." "True civilization," he cried, "is not to be found in gas, steam, or railroad turntables. It consists in the diminution of the traces of original sin." [17]

Baudelaire's preoccupation with sin had little to do with conventional theology and was actually a mystically staged form of suffering stemming from the romantic tradition of a personally inherited "curse." Beyond that, it served as a way of stating questions of "depth" and forcing them dramatically on the imagination of his readers. But if his theological and moral orthodoxy were not literal, his cultural anti-secularism was. As Barbey d'Aurevilly said of him, speaking as a Catholic, "he has nothing of our faith, of our respects, but he has our hatreds and repugnances." [18] Baudelaire hated those who believed that science would reveal all to men. He hated democracy and equality and those who believed that these would make a better world. He hated a trust in technology which assumed that technology, bringing power and comfort, would also bring happiness. He hated modern values because they were explicit and optimistic, and he felt as others felt in his time—and as some, perhaps many, still do—that this explicitness and optimism were in some way philosophically and morally vulgar. In this sense, he was an enemy of modern secularism, and his outlook was religious because it demanded a retention of the uncontrollable in human affairs and the philosophical anxiety and aesthetic intrigue of the world.

For Baudelaire, Flaubert, and Stendhal, a discussion of modern culture unavoidably converged on the middle class as the chief instrument of modern values. But the responses to this realization were tinged with their different tempers. Flaubert was always vindictive and Baudelaire fervently tortured, whereas Stendhal managed a studied distance mixed with a kind of repelled interest. Such well-contrived skepticism, he felt, kept the observer from being morally or intellectually abused by social reality and turned inquiry into a game of gratification for the curious. He was, as he put in the title of one of his books, a "tourist," a transient witness, a seeker of special experience. His whole life may be called a continuous, deliberate, almost disciplined pursuit of intellectual and sensual pleasure. This explains why he regarded the work regimen instituted by the bourgeoisie as a profound menace to the expansion of the personality and the free art of enjoying life. During his visit to Geneva, Stendhal was struck by what the spirit of industriousness could do to the happiness of people. Like others after him, he believed that there was some connection between the Protestant personality and business acumen—love of money, he wrote, was "the great lesson of Calvinism." But he noticed that acquisitive skill did not beget any pleasurable use of the wealth it created. On the contrary, it imposed such a forbidding discipline upon the life of the Calvinist that, he said, "any happy Genevan would be run out of town." [19] Not only did the business spirit diminish the prospects of happiness. It undermined the proper basis of the social order. Businessmen did not distinguish between their rising material power and its legitimate function. They had, so to speak, failed "to keep their place." Industrialists had undoubtedly made France a stronger country. They were good, honest men. But they were not "admirable" men—a lawyer, a doctor, or an architect—and it should be regarded as unthinkable to put businessmen in a position to judge the achievements of writers and scientists, as the Saint-Simonians had proposed. Were the talents of great poets and savants to be sanctioned by "the general assembly of masons, rope-makers, or the members of the privileged classes like My Lord Baron Rothschild and his retinue?" [20]

When Stendhal conceded to businessmen their being "honest" men he may have been reviving the old French notion of the merchant as "honneste personne," the only one among the ordinary people to be regarded as respectable in recognition of his public usefulness. Certainly this is all he would have granted, because his view of social hierarchy was so completely the product of intellectual virtues that it dismissed without question the entire history of rank and occupational distinctions elaborated by the bourgeoisie. For him all persons engaged in the machinery of production, whether artisans or financiers, belonged to the same group by virtue of their motivations and their capabilities. They were all dealers in things, thing-handlers and thing-makers, inherently disqualified to render decisions in which the higher aims of men were at stake.

This paradoxical article of faith, that the very class which had successfully assumed power in the course of a social and political revolution was to be declared morally and culturally out of bounds, has a history which goes deeper than many of the nineteenth-century intellectuals suspected. In his analysis of the French chronicles of the fifteenth century, Johan Huizinga found that court writers would conveniently neglect the actual weight of the bourgeoisie in French society in order to retain a stereotyped portrayal of the traditional order of repute. For these writers the nobility was the sole embodiment of veracity, courage, and largesse. To the noblemen were naturally entrusted the highest functions of the state, the defense of the church, and the safeguard of the people. No distinction was to be drawn between the meanest laborer and the wealthiest merchant, both of whom were equally relegated to the Third Estate, unworthy of the chronicler's attention as "hardly capable of high attributes and being only of servile condition." [21] Another social historian, Bernhard Groethuysen, looking at French church records of the eighteenth century, found in them a radical social dualism in ethical life which put the bourgeoisie in a spiritually empty middle between the extremes of the nobility and the humble. According to the Gospels there were in the world two forms of greatness: the greatness of power and the greatness of poverty. The privileges of the powerful were an emanation of God, who was the greatest among lords and who had charged them with the duty to lift nations to the level of their own magnificence. The moral greatness of the poor, "the image of Christ crucified by us," lay in the living parable of their own humility. One class was, so to speak, Godlike and the other Christlike, but both belonged to the transcendental order of things and revealed in their lives great teachings and great purpose. The bourgeois, on the other hand, were neither poor nor powerful (power-filled) in the ancestral sense. They had neither the spiritual magnificence of the *seigneur* nor the Christlike resignation of the humble. Everything they did was cautious, limited, and perceptible in its rewards and ends. Their lives were normal and, for that reason, had no larger meaning and said nothing about man's destiny.[22]*

This picture of historical morality (taking morality in the medieval sense of spiritual instruction dramatically conveyed by symbolic portraits of the social order) is absent from secular writers. But these found other ways of underscoring the spiritual inferiority of the middle class. The Duke of Saint-Simon, for example, thought it disgraceful that Louis XIV should engage the famous banker Samuel Bernard in friendly conversation.[23] And later in the eighteenth century, Duclos regarded it as a matter worth special notice that "quite a few polished gen-

* The philosopher Montesquieu came from an old-style provincial noble family. According to a story, a beggar who happened to knock at the door shortly after Montesquieu's birth was asked to be the child's godfather so that the child might remember his obligations to the poor in later life. Aynard, *op. cit.*, p. 347.

tlemen could be found among financiers." [24] According to Voltaire, everyone in France tried to be an aristocrat by holding the merchants in contempt, while the merchant, "by dint of hearing his profession despised on all occasions, at least is fool enough to blush at his condition." [25] It is true that the ambitious bourgeois dreamed of getting his children into the bureaucracy or the professions and that he sometimes looked on the shopkeeper as inferior and barely above the general population. We may presume, however, that Voltaire was using "merchant" in the general sense of "businessman" because we know that money, even in great amounts, could not reconcile the bourgeois to the lack of cultural and ancestral pedigree. Few rich people, according to Duclos, failed to experience the humiliation of being considered as "nothing but wealthy." [26] Mme. d'Epinay said of a financier's wife: "She was a woman who was somewhat hard and proud, who displayed her wealth, but who nevertheless was inconsolable about being nothing but a financier's wife." [27] Toward the end of the Old Regime, Beaumarchais denounced the dramatic convention which depicted the middle class as insignificant and ridiculous, for the fact is that not even among its own intellectual friends could the bourgeoisie gain an autonomous prestige. Middle-class characters had found a place in eighteenth-century domestic drama, but when the great political moment of the middle class, the Revolution, finally arrived, no one could think of the means to render it heroic. Instead, authors of revolutionary plays resorted to parading the new political virtues in ancient toga.[28] The bourgeoisie, Marx said, engineered the transformation of modern society in the midst of mock reconstruction of the Roman Republic.[29]

The surprising realization that emerges from this is that the attack of the nineteenth-century intellectuals upon the bourgeoisie is, in effect, a continuation of the earlier debate about the social-moral role of the middle class. Louis Blanc said that the bourgeois were too devoid of grandeur to urge extreme courses. De Tocqueville held that either the aristocracy or the people could bring some great purpose to society, but that the bourgeoisie could never go beyond an order "without virtue and without grandeur." [30] In the intellectual tradition the bourgeoisie was, therefore, the secular class—the profane class in the spiritual sense—lacking the will to greatness and incapable of philosophical or epochal glamor. "Far be it from me to conclude that industrialists are not honorable," explained Stendhal. "All I mean is that they are not heroic." [31]

NOTES TO CHAPTER VIII

1. Cited in Erich Auerbach, *Mimesis* (New York: Doubleday Anchor Books, 1957), p. 354.

2. Karl Marx, *The Communist Manifesto*.

3. Sartre, *op. cit.*, p. 104; Pierre Flottes, *Baudelaire* (Perrin et Cie., 1955), pp. 60-61, 82.

4. Charles Baudelaire, *Oeuvres complètes* (6 vols.; Paris: Éditions de la Nouvelle Revue Française, 1923), **IV**, 76.

5. Cited in Francis Steegmuller, *Flaubert and Madame Bovary* (London: Collins, 1947), p. 303.

6. Stendhal, *The Life of Henri Brulard* (New York: Vintage Books, 1955), pp. 60-61, 82.

7. Gustave Flaubert, *Correspondance* (5 vols.; Paris: Louis Conard, 1810), **II**, 25.

8. Charles Baudelaire, *Intimate Journals,* trans. Christopher Isherwood, intro. W. H. Auden (Hollywood: Marcel Rodd, 1947), p. 75.

9. Stendhal, *Memoirs of Egotism,* Matthew Josephson, ed. (New York: Lear Publishers, 1949), p. 120; Gustave Flaubert, *Selected Letters,* trans. and ed. Francis Steegmuller (New York: Farrar, Strauss & Young, Inc., 1953), p. 264; Stendhal, *Memoirs of Egotism,* p. 151.

10. Cited in Steegmuller, *Flaubert and Madame Bovary,* pp. 34-35.

11. Baudelaire, *Intimate Journals,* p. 67.

12. Stendhal, *Mémoires d'un touriste* (3 vols.; Paris: Le Divan, 1929), **I**, 48.

13. Stendhal, *Mélanges de littérature* (3 vols.; Paris: Le Divan, 1933), **II**, 249.

14. Flaubert, *Correspondance,* **IV**, 53, 329.

15. Baudelaire, *Oeuvres complètes,* **IV**, 53.

16. Cited in Joseph D. Bennett, *Baudelaire: A Criticism* (Princeton: Princeton University Press, 1944), p. 15.

17. Baudelaire, *Oeuvres complètes,* **VI**, 424.

18. Cited in Flottes, *op. cit.,* p. 66.

19. Stendhal, *Mémoires d'un touriste,* **III**, 66, 52.

20. Stendhal, *Mélanges de littérature,* **II**, 217-229.

21. Johan Huizinga, *The Waning of the Middle Ages* (London: Edward Arnold & Co., 1924), pp. 48-50.

22. Bernhard Groethuysen, *Origines de l'esprit bourgeois en France* (2 vols.; Paris: Gallimard, 1927), **I**, 165-176.

23. Duke de Saint-Simon, *Memoirs on the Reign of Louis XIV and the Regency* (3 vols.; London: Bickers and Sons), **II**, 17.

24. Glotz and Marie, *op. cit.,* p. 18.

25. Voltaire, *op. cit.,* **XXXIX**, 18.

26. Barber, *op. cit.,* p. 57.

27. *Ibid.,* p. 57.

28. Plekhanov, *Art and Society* (New York: Critics Group, 1936), pp. 16-17.

29. Marx, *The Eighteenth Brumaire of Louis Napoleon,* p. 11.

30. De Tocqueville, *Recollections,* p. 6.

31. Stendhal, *Mélanges de littérature,* **II**, 227.

CHAPTER IX

THE FANATICISM
OF UTENSILS: BOURGEOIS
CULTURE AS MASS CULTURE

"FOR ONE MAN to judge another," wrote Flaubert, "is a spectacle that could make me die laughing if it did not inspire me with pity." [1] In this, as in other statements, Flaubert intended that mixture of hilarity and bitterness which he regarded as the only appropriate response to the moral pretensions of his contemporaries. Besides that he wanted to remind himself and others that socially oriented ideas were senseless because social experience was itself senseless. Intellectuals, therefore, as a point of integrity and, indeed, of rationality, should refuse to adopt a "responsible" attitude toward others.

Flaubert's irritation with the "spectacle" of moral judgment had two sources. One was a judgment of his own that other people's piety is hypocrisy. The other was that moral discussion represents a degree of social flexibility which foolishly endangers social discipline. Flaubert's public views can be very puzzling if one looks only at the surface of his remarks. His breezy impatience and his scandalized amusement at modern society suggests that he had no serious concern for it. The boundless fury which society could also arouse in him suggests that society was his dominant preoccupation. Actually both things are true, for Flaubert's great hope was to have the question of social order settled once and for all through a collective principle so rigid that moralizing by groups or individuals would become superfluous. He gave two reasons for this: first that moral argument could not be recognized as a general privilege because certain provinces of society (such as the intellectual elite) were above the moral judgment of others, and, second, that all true values were, by definition, fixed and could emanate only from a fixed social system.

Why the stability of values should have concerned Flaubert and others so greatly is a matter which illuminates still another corner of the bourgeois question. Their profound conviction was that "meaningful" values stood for stable values, and "meaningful" values were by definition nonutilitarian values. The middle class, however, was the vanguard of the utilitarian spirit, and this caused de Tocqueville to say that a moral order could only come from the aristocracy or the people. De Tocqueville was writing as a political man and an intellectual aristocrat trying to discover the possibilities of cultural dignity in the forthcoming democratic era. Other observers had neither his political interests nor his hopes, but they shared his view of culture, which may be said to rest on the aesthetic completeness or incompleteness of cultural structures. According to this view, "true" cultural reality has both integrity and depth and for this reason can be possessed only by an individual who is himself a finished universe of intellectual and aesthetic principles or by a culture which stands as a harmonious monument to custom, belief, and symbol. The bourgeoisie, on the other hand, seemed to be inherently valueless and cultureless because the content of its life lacked definition, boundaries, self-containment, and, therefore, intrinsic worth. This is what accounted for both its worldly success and its spiritual misery. Bourgeois culture was typically expansive (and everyone was eager to embrace its canons of material possessiveness and contentment and was capable of doing so) because its values were essentially extensible, which is to say that they were essentially depthless and exchangeable and could be transmitted through market transactions ("in bourgeois society," said Baudelaire, "everyone is a second-hand dealer," adding ironically, "even the rich").[2] It is impossible to insist on these distinctions too much. For the literary enemies of modernity, qualitative cultural reality was always specific cultural reality. Bourgeois life was condemned to reproduce itself in a qualitative vacuum, as Stendhal had implicitly contended by refusing to differentiate between a shoemaker and a banking potentate. It did not echo the spirit of a true culture. It did not challenge the person's "real" being, nor was it an assertion or an expansion of that being. For that reason the bourgeoisie, no matter how selfish, would always be lacking in individuality, like that Baudelairian epitome of the shopkeeper's civilization, the Belgian merchants, who could "only think in partnership." [3] All market activities constituted spiritually debilitating acts and should be exposed and resisted precisely because, under bourgeois guidance, the total life of society was becoming more and more identified with the processes of production and consumption. The other side of economic competition and success, Flaubert wrote, was always an extension of uniformity and a reduction of the creative faculties, "a permanent conspiracy against originality." [4]

Accounts of the French bourgeoisie in the early and middle parts of the nineteenth century offer the picture of a class marked by great ambitions and awkward pretentions. Its chief cultural feature was an upstart punctilio about being "well informed," which, combined with a lack of intellectual discrimination, made it susceptible to faddist enthusiasms. Its overriding social preoccupation was to "arrive" by purchasing its way into acceptability and acquiring the accepted graces. *Paris et les parisiens,* one of the several chronicles of French mores to appear during the Orleanist period, describes the social tactics of a wealthy baker as follows: first, exchange of the white apron for a black coat; second, finishing school for his daughter where she will learn "the subjunctive and the piano"; third, pass the word to socially prominent bachelors that the young woman's dowry is an irresistible million francs.[5]

Crass and pathetic as the spectacle of bourgeois climbing may have been, it was not necessarily a threatening one. Yet, Stendhal and Flaubert could speak of it only with venom and alarm. There was for them something outrageous about a century in which "a poor devil [made] a hundred thousand francs," the rabble crowded the public places, bootblacks aspired to be bootmakers, and valets to be masters.[6] But why? Obviously because utility, progress, equality, vulgarity, and intellectual desolation were inextricably bound together. It was not merely that the masses were incapable of leadership, "born fire-worshipers" or "eternal minors," though they certainly were this.[7] It was not their lack of grace or cultural poise, for, to the literary taste of this time (and, indeed, of ours) brutality was far preferable to vulgarity. Stendhal, for one, while disliking uncleanliness, did not mind it so much among the populace of Rome because there it was at least "hidden by ferocity." [8] The terrible thing was the transformation of popular simplemindedness into what Baudelaire called "general avarice," the spreading to all classes of the desire for gain as the means of social repute.

Among democratic nations ambition is ardent and continual, but its aims are not habitually lofty; and life is generally spent in eagerly coveting small objects that are within reach.

What chiefly diverts men of democracies from lofty ambitions is not the scantiness of their fortunes, but the vehemence of the exertions they daily make to improve them. They strain their faculties to the utmost to achieve paltry results, and this cannot fail speedily to limit their range of view and circumscribe their power. They might be poorer and still be greater.[9]

For de Tocqueville, this was the consequence of the political
and economic dissolution of the old class differences. He had
very little of the eighteenth-century confidence in the individual to summon a meaningful universe by the power of single-
handed rationality. He thought that, deprived of a model of
public behavior and a "self-image" issuing from a traditional
group style of existence, the individual would be forced to
"make himself," which meant in effect that he would enter
the race for acquisition as the only instrument of self-
expression. What de Tocqueville was saying and what the anti-
market literary view maintained, was that a socially rising but
cultureless person had no choice but to be economically aggres-
sive. What Stendhal, Flaubert, and Baudelaire saw beyond that,
however, was that besides being the ruling class the bourgeoisie
constituted, paradoxically, the model for democratic aspirations
in de Tocqueville's sense. The bourgeois may exploit their
fellow citizens, but they had nothing against the masses sharing
in bourgeois ambitions, because these ambitions were, psychologically, intellectually, and morally transferable to everyone.
The bourgeoisie was the first ruling class in history whose
values could be acquired by all classes, and bourgeois culture
was, in this sense, the first true democratic culture.

A great deal has been said by historians and sociologists
about the destruction of personal relationships with the introduction of industrial competition into European life. De Tocqueville, for instance, saw as one of the chief wrongs of
manufacturing society that the employer represented only the
agency of economic rewards and duties and no longer the human face of a traditional social bond. Literary men were
equally concerned with the moral emptiness of industrial existence, but with obvious and significant differences. They did
not as much worry about the person-to-person relations as to
the person himself. Which is to say that, for them, the question
of personality was psychologically a more intricate and absolute
one. The issue was this: the compelling sameness of modern

market-place experience would irresistibly weld the world into
massive and ever greater human indistinctiveness. And this
left nothing to genuine individuals but to become "total" individuals and to refuse all invitations to membership in the
social surroundings. There is a paragraph in Flaubert which
appears to complain about incidentals, but actually leads to
the heart of the matter.

Seamstresses and tailors no longer know anything about costuming,
nor upholsterers about furnishings, nor cooks about cuisine. The reasons are the same that cause portrait painters to paint poor portraits. . . . The narrow specialization within which they live does
away with the very meaning of that specialization and they constantly take the accessory for the principal. . . . A great tailor
could be an artist as, in the 16th century, goldsmiths were artists; but
mediocrity infiltrates everything. Even stones have become mediocre
and the new big highways are dull. Let us be determined to perish
(and we shall perish, rest assured), but, let us by all possible means
stand in the way of the *merde* which envelops us. Let us enlist ourselves in the cause of the ideal. Since we no longer have the means
of dwelling in marble halls and covering ourselves with the purple,
to rest upon divans stuffed with hummingbird feathers, to step on
swansdown carpets, sit in mahogany armchairs . . . or to read by
emerald-encrusted lamps, let us cry against imitation silk, desk chairs,
economy kitchens, fake materials, fake luxury, fake pride. Indus-
trialism has developed the ugly to gigantic proportions. . . . The
department store has rendered true luxury difficult . . . we have all
become fakers and charlatans; pose, pose and humbug everywhere.
. . . Our century is a whorish century . . . the least prostituted
are the real prostitutes.[10]

At first this passage seems to suffer from certain odd and
strained juxtapositions, such as Flaubert's appeal to the ideal
as a means of combating the cultural effects of the department
store. But let us re-examine it by asking certain questions. Why
take up the cry against imitation silk? Why join the battle
against fake luxury? The reason, he says, is that it leads to fake
pride. One must conclude from this that true pride is con-
nected with and sustained by true luxury (and vice versa) and

that it is legitimate, while fake pride is not. The point is simply and frankly that the inaccessibility of certain possessions (poetically exalted by Flaubert as swandown carpets and sofas stuffed with hummingbird feathers) made for well-defined barriers in social condition. Mass-produced clothing and the availability of spurious objects of art tended to dim social lines which, in turn, led to the deterioration of manners. And manners were, after all, the visible sign of a sound social hierarchy in which the exhibition of pure cultural traits corresponded to the possession of social power. Formerly, the fashion had been set by well-established social groups. But now there was an "anarchy of social appearance," which violated the symbolic function of dress as an expression of personal character and the social order needed for a civilized existence. Flaubert intended to uphold these principles even at the cost of lonesome eccentricity—he would, he said, continue to wear top hats and houserobes. Perhaps it was the same logic that led Victor Hugo to develop his infatuation with expensive wardrobes ("Enter the lords superbly dressed," read the stage directions for the first act of *Le Roi s'amuse*), a taste which the *Comédie française* eventually found impossible to finance.[12] According to *Les Français peints par eux-mêmes,* the man of letters, once the vassal of the nobility and the crown, had taken to play king himself by surrounding his life with the antiquarian splendors of old china, medieval tapestries, carved furniture, and ancient panoplies.[13]

But again, how can one understand Flaubert's curious leap in tone which suddenly calls for a defense of the "ideal" while decrying the fall of elegance? Here are his words once more: "Let us enlist ourselves in the cause of the ideal since we no longer have the means of dwelling in marble halls and covering ourselves with the purple. . . ." The point is quite clear. In the absence of the social discipline represented by a true aristocracy (that is, one representing spiritual excellence and having the power to enforce it) and in the face of a democratized

fakery of aristocratic possessions, the new intellectual aristocracy must devise cultural means of asserting itself. Pure intellectual symbolism was to take the place of the old social symbolism of possessions. In an economically mobile society the
intellectual must retain his identity and his position by making
ideas inaccessible to the masses. Since goods and even luxuries
were now available to them, thought and art should be made
rare, precious and, in their own way, expensive.

Louis Philippe's government, like all modern governments,
regarded road-building as a basic article of policy; and thousands of miles of new roads were constructed during his reign in
the interest of an expanding trade. Flaubert's sole reaction to
these signs of progress was to say that the new roads were big
and tedious and that now even paving stones had become bor-
ing. Hundreds of utterances as to what is psychologically and
aesthetically wrong with modern society are embraced in this
observation. Two meanings, both negative, are lodged within
the word "big." One is the idea of public numbers, of the many,
what Ortega y Gasset calls *el lleno,* the "full-house" atmosphere of the modern world.[14] The other is the idea of one-
dimensionality. The two meanings are, in fact, related. Anything which is public, available to numbers, must be readily
used by them. The new highways were meant for the greater
flow of traffic; they consolidated public movement into one
single-directed stream, large-scale and unremitting. They had
no room for retreat, for hidden experience, no distraction
from explicit purpose, and their "obviousness" and monotony
were the indispensable consequence of their usefulness. Useful,
therefore, emerges out of this reasoning as the antithesis of
personal, an opposition which Flaubert saw at work in every
aspect of contemporary motivation and social experience. The
naked clarity of a mechanized existence paralleled the easily
measurable wants of the market place and the surrender of
intimacy to the satisfaction of collective needs. Modern society
was an eminently public society. Baudelaire was obsessed by

this realization. He saw "something base" in all public functions and said that *fonctionnaires* (which for him meant state ministers, newspaper editors, and theater managers) who, in some way, had to act as servants of public expectations, could only do so by becoming "persons without personality" and traitors to an original inward life.[15]

In a public culture what was its protagonist, the public, like? All three writers used the term "masses" and, at least two of them, Stendhal and Flaubert, did so in a way not essentially different from that of contemporary sociological usage. The mass man for them appeared out of the destruction of specific historical loyalties. Corporate forms of social existence had been destroyed, and men could no longer apprehend society in a distinct and concrete way. As Flaubert put it with aphoristic bitterness, 1789 had destroyed the aristocracy, 1848 the bourgeoisie, and 1851 the people. Now only the mob remained.[16] Stendhal attributed the presence of mass attitudes to the big cities and to the dependence of their inhabitants upon impersonal means of communication. It was not only that the size of the community kept men from appropriating social experience first-hand. A habit of social distance and indirection had actually developed, even toward events which occurred within reach so that, as Stendhal said, a man going by a house where something unusual had happened would rather wait for the account of next day's newspapers than to look in the window. The fundamental difference between Paris and a village was that the village trusted that it could understand its life directly, whereas Paris saw everything "through the dailies." [17]

The presence of the masses involved two questions, the political and the cultural. Stendhal seems to have looked at the two questions separately, though it is difficult to extract one consistent view from his various statements. Culturally his verdict was quite decisive; the masses were one of the "great evils of civilization, and a threat to arts and letters." [18] They had "political advantages" but, whatever was meant by this (and it may have been no more than his way of describing their malleability as tools for politicians), it is clear that Stendhal was not the Jacobin holdout in an age of bourgeois conformity that some critics would have him be.[19] Stendhal sometimes claimed his opinions to be "entirely and fundamentally republican." But we know that he used such words as taunts aimed at provincial windbags and stuffed shirts, or as elaborate gestures of defiance toward his family; he confessed that he decided to embrace republican sentiments because his household was so snobbish. Actually, of course, Stendhal was the exponent of an adroitly nurtured snobbery of his own according to which genuine political republicanism was "the real cholera morbus" and a horrible condition anywhere except in America. The intention of the latter remark is not clear. Perhaps it meant that the New World operated under a special dispensation. Perhaps (remembering what other French men of letters thought of the United States) it meant that it should be given up for lost and left to the barbarians. At any rate, Stendhal's rightful place is with the not unfamiliar company of intellectuals who, contemptuous of rulers and wishing only the best for the "people," could never have endured one minute of the people's life. As a youth he went to the Jacobin Club of Grenoble thinking of himself as a Cincinnatus and thrilling at the social and political adventure of such dare. He found the people wretched and the place vile, and he left faced with the inescapable fact of his aristocratic instincts. Somewhat unconvincingly he once wrote that he would do "anything" for the happiness of the people. But, he added more truthfully perhaps, that he would rather pass a fortnight out of every month in jail than to live with them. "I abhor the mob," he said elsewhere with unconcealed finality.[20]

The question of the masses as a dangerous cultural condition kept Flaubert and Stendhal in a constant state of contempt and alarm. They were, of course, not the only writers to react in this way, but they were among the most unforgiving and the most perceptive. According to Flaubert, the conspiracy of contentment and materialistic enthusiasm which had gripped modern society—"the fever of moral abasement," [21]—were all creations of the masses, and no concession could be made to them that would not constitute a surrender of "values" to the imperium of wants. In the case of Baudelaire, some of his fury at popular vulgarity occasionally took very unexpected turns. Being a man who constantly hungered for originality and the *outré,* he might be suspected of a sporting sympathy for such defiers of the social order as the anarchist. Actually he considered the anarchist as nothing more than another mass man, another cultural equalitarian, "an enemy of art, of perfume, a fanatic of utensils." [22] In fact, he took the side of the paid servant of the established order, the policeman, whom he admonished to strike "religiously" at the anarchist's back. We may ignore Baudelaire's championing of perfume as too manneristic to enlist approval or win understanding. But we should notice his coupling of popular aspirations with the "fanaticism of utensils." For him, as for Flaubert, democracy, like the bourgeois spirit which constituted its nurturing force, was nothing but the cultural façade for the powers of "iron, steam, and wheelwork," which dominated the modern world—a psychological contrivance to foster the external and to cater to the external.[23] Hatred of the bourgeois was, therefore, "the beginning of all virtue." But more still. Because bourgeois ambitions had now penetrated to every class, this hatred must be extended to "all humanity, including the people." [24] The great revolution of our time was something far deeper than public institutions or political practices. It was a revolution of the psychological and emotional fabric, of the quality of life. It was, Flaubert said, "the raising of the working class to the level of stupidity attained by the bourgeoisie." [25]

NOTES TO CHAPTER IX

1. Flaubert, *Correspondance*, I, 101.
2. Baudelaire, *Oeuvres complètes*, VI, 437.
3. *Ibid.*, p. 436.
4. Flaubert, *Correspondance*, I, 281.
5. Alexandre Dumas, Théophile Gautier, *et al.*, *Paris et les parisiens au XIXᵉ siècle* (Paris: Laplace, Sanchez et Cie.), pp. 426-427.
6. Stendhal, *Mémoires d'un touriste*, III, 25; Flaubert, *Selected Letters*, pp. 21-22.
7. Baudelaire, *Intimate Journals*, p. 38; Flaubert, *Correspondance*, IV, 61.
8. Stendhal, *Mémoires d'un touriste*, I, 22.
9. De Tocqueville, *Democracy in America*, II, 245.
10. Flaubert, *Correspondance*, II, 427-428.
11. *Ibid.*, II, 428-429.
12. F. W. Draper, *op. cit.*, p. 291.
13. *Les Français*, VIII, 226.
14. José Ortega y Gasset, *La Rebelión de las Masas* (Buenos Aires-Mexico: Espasa Calpe, 1944), pp. 41 f.
15. Bennet, *op. cit.*, p. 7; Charles Baudelaire, *The Essence of Laughter*, ed. Peter Quennell (New York: Meridian Books, 1956), p. 181.
16. Flaubert, *Correspondance*, II, 336.
17. Stendhal, *Mémoires d'un touriste*, I, 40.
18. *Ibid.*, I, 40.
19. Stendhal, *Mémoires of Egotism*, Introduction, p. 7.
20. Stendhal, *The Life of Henri Brulard* (New York: Vintage, 1955), pp. 129, 135, 209.
21. Flaubert, *Correspondance*, II, 336.
22. Cited in Flottes, *Baudelaire*, p. 50.
23. Flaubert, *Correspondance*, II, 281.
24. Cited in Steegmuller, *Flaubert and Madame Bovary*, p. 250.
25. Cited in Philip Spencer, *Flaubert: A Biography* (New York: Grove Press, 1952), p. 190.

CHAPTER X

THE ATTACK ON THE
SOCIAL, ECONOMIC, AND
PSYCHOLOGICAL OPTIMISM
OF MODERN SOCIETY

IN *Democracy in America* de Tocqueville says:

The greater part of the men who constitute these [democratic] nations are extremely eager in the pursuit of actual and physical gratifications. As they are always dissatisfied with the position that they
occupy and are always free to leave it, they think of nothing but the
means of changing their fortune or increasing it. To minds thus pre-
disposed, every new method that leads by a shorter road to wealth,
every machine that spares labor, every instrument that diminishes
the cost of production, every discovery that facilitates pleasures or
augments them, seems to be the grandest effort of the human intellect. It is chiefly from these motives that a democratic people addicts
itself to scientific pursuits, that it understands and respects them. In
aristocratic ages science is more particularly called upon to furnish
gratification to the mind; in democracy, to the body.[1]

Both Flaubert and Baudelaire looked into the heart of the
democratic prospect and decided that it must be opposed by at-
tacking every philosophy of social "improvement" and every
method of making that doctrine reality. Flaubert's words on

this question seemed mild enough at times—a patient reminder of such traditional themes as the impermanence of things and the timelessness of life, or amusement over the naïve confidence of utopians that a perfect society could be sprung intellectually in short order. Actually, the depth of revulsion which he and Baudelaire felt before the dreams of progress and the inroads of democracy can only be measured by the fact that they chose as their stand nothing less than the ancient doctrine of the natural depravity of man. Flaubert thought that the dogma of equality was propounded against every evidence of history and psychology; for Baudelaire progress was absurd because, whether in the jungle or on the boulevard, man remained a predatory animal. The hopes for man were, at best, to make the beast a little less vicious.[2] The ideological function of this argument moved in three directions. The first, and most obvious, was that it denied all meaning to material progress, thus placing the question of advance on the spiritual plane where the literary mind wanted to have it. Second, while maintaining the evilness of Man, it held possible the excellence of individuals. This reinforced the case for an intellectual elite with an added suggestion of the orthodox doctrine of personally attained grace as the only means to overcome sinfulness. Finally, in regarding depravity as ineradicable, Baudelaire and Flaubert's argument provided moral sanction for their political and social indifference.

Although Stendhal had profited from the ascension of Bonaparte, his repugnance for the quality of modern mass uplifting led him at times to regret the passing of the Old Regime. "Try and imagine," he once wrote, "the joy which anteceded the rise of the passions of 1789."[3] The statement was directed at the noisome strain which Stendhal saw in all ideologies of wholesale regeneration. It was also an attack on the officious impatience with which the zealots of reform looked on the shortcomings of the human race. This made such people a threat to any sane and comforting adjustment to the inescapable predicaments of life. They also attacked sensuality in which man had always found a compensation for life's trials.

For Flaubert, particularly, most of the political teachings of the "philosophico-evangelical vermin," as he called the Saint-Simonians, Comtians, and other social writers, was only another form of materialistic pietism. These prophets were not only philistine. They were vicious. Their outlook might be secular, even ostentatiously nonreligious, but their minds were essentially sectarian, magisterial, "fundamentalistic"—in fact, unachronistic. They were a novel breed of pedestrian fanatics ("bookkeepers in delirium"), afire with the trivial vision of satisfying mass appetites and the fearful one of destroying "all individual initiative, all personality and all thought." [4] Flaubert had no doubt that, in the hands of the compulsive reformer, the state would become an omnipotent force:

a sort of monster . . . which will direct everything, do everything. A sacerdotal tyranny is at the bottom of these narrow hearts. "It is necessary to regulate everything to refashion everything, to put everything on a new basis." There is no nonsense, no vice which will not find its blueprinters and its dreamers. I believe that man has never been as fanatical as today.[5]

Once in a while, in the course of these attacks, Flaubert would revive the memory of the French Revolution and its heritage of freedom, but this must be taken as a rhetorical stimulant for his denunciations rather than a serious argument for political liberties. This becomes clear by simply looking at the philosophical premises of the Revolution. For the eighteenth century the individual had been the analytically demonstrable reality from which social generalization could be derived. It was the locus of reason, freedom, and virtue—the seed from which rational, free, and just social relations grew. Self-love, Morelly said, was by nature indissolubly bound with benevolence and hence played the same role in social life that the law of gravity played in Newton's physical world. For Helvetius and Holbach, nature had so constructed man that he could not be happy without other men, and without making *them* happy. In 1789 Sieyès stated that "les volontés individuelles sont les seuls elements de la volonté commune." [6] In saying this he was reaffirming the Rousseaunian belief that a free, rational, and sovereign society was the sum total of naturally free, rational, and sovereign individuals brought into social partnership through the agency of the general will.

Flaubert was a belligerent stranger to all of this. For one thing he shared with the romantics the refusal to assign specific meaning to the idea of cause. Individuals, nations, culture, and historical events were from this point of view treated as unique phenomena to be understood not by cognition, but by empathy, intuition, or aesthetic identification. This explains the unexpected tie between the literary and the political forms of romanticism. Social romanticism was a revival of political traditionalism, neo-feudal at times, decrying social fragmentation and exalting an unspoiled sense of community born of spontaneous loyalty to ritualized custom. At first, of course, nothing seems more inimical to this than literary individualism, which is always unequivocally egotistical and demands everything for the individual as it expects everything from it. Actually the two are founded on a rejection of what Mannheim calls the "mechanical thought model," that is, a style of thinking which assumes all events and ideas to be unambiguously measurable and describable. Political and social romanticism rejected the mechanistic model in favor of organicism, the belief in the unbroken fabric of the traditional community. Literary romanticism rejected the same model in the name of personalism, the belief in the uniqueness of individual gifts. In both cases, however, the principle depended on the assumption of an unassailable, whole, and living reality.

Flaubert, as well as Baudelaire, stood equally apart from the rationalistic individualism of the Enlightenment, the somewhat cabalistic individualism of the early literary romantics and the ceremonial group-feelings of the political romantics. Their re-

jection of rationalistic individualism should be obvious enough;
it is just this kind of rationalism that is at the root of all modern
optimistic social views. Their dislike for the early romantics
had somewhat different sources. Baudelaire disliked them because his rather natty sense of decorum was offended by their
theatricality. Flaubert disliked them because he thought that
they were given to consoling themselves with reverie and momentary emotion instead of toughening themselves to the nasti-
ness of their surroundings. For a moment the philosophical
pessimism of these two writers and their opposition to planned
reform might suggest the conservative label. But this, too, would
be doubtful. Conservatism was a political position, a theory of
social bonds, an invitation to participate in certain communal
duties and opportunities. And this they both religiously refused. They had, on the other hand, a great many things to say
about the wisdom of indifference, and the dangers and vices of
modern ideology. From this, three peculiar views of public action emerge: political violence as a form of aesthetic excitement, autocracy, and magical hero-worship.

There are, for Flaubert and Baudelaire, two sides to the political question, one farcical and one clinical. The first has to
do with the garrulous and explosive nonsense of political illusions. The second has to do with the application of pure power
as a social preventive. Writing with evident delight Baudelaire
observed that, although bizarreness was the rule in the political
life of Latin America, there "at least people kill each other." [7] In
the same spirit, Flaubert claimed that of all public occur-
rences the only one he could appreciate was the riot. While both
of these statements echo with a certain romantic fondness for
excess, they really express the aesthetic side of social cynicism.
Pragmatic human events were of no cultural interest because
they reflected only the monotonous drone of the daily utilitarian
rounds. The thing to do, therefore, was to isolate extraordinary
happenings as an amusing (even when bloody) side show to
be observed for its dramatic touches or interesting aberra-

tions. It was in obedience to this doctrine that Flaubert and a friend came to Paris at the outbreak of the revolution of 1848 to look at it "from the artistic point of view." [8] The two went about the city investigating street fighting, dined pleasantly at a good restaurant, and sat the night reading poetry some three hundred yards from the scene of some of the bloodiest episodes of the revolt. Baudelaire's behavior is somewhat mystifying, but still very private. He joined the crowds in the streets but apparently did nothing more than wander around shouting "Shoot General Aupick." [9] * The subject of this curious slogan was his stepfather, whom he detested as a competitor for his mother's affection and as a vulgarian incapable of understanding a poet's emotional or economic troubles.

It is true that Baudelaire seemed, for a while, to become interested in the condition of the French working class, at least to the extent of writing for a minor left-wing publication, and contributing a preface to a book of "proletarian" poetry (Pierre Dupont's *Chansons*) in which he spoke of the workers as the oppressed producers of wealth who would inherit the earth. Pierre Flotte, one of Baudelaire's biographers, sees all of this as no more than grist for the poet's showy rebelliousness, but George Plekhanov, seeking an opening for Marxist interpretation, says that Baudelaire relapsed into literary egotism only because of the victory of counterrevolutionary forces in 1852. [10]

---

* A contemporary witness who ran into Baudelaire in the streets on the twenty-fourth of February 1848, gives the following account:

> I found him at night in the midst of a mob that had just raided an armory. He was carrying a beautiful, shining and immaculate-looking rifle. He came towards me simulating great agitation and said, "I have just fired a shot." I smiled seeing the brand-new appearance of the weapon and remarked, "Not for the Republic?" He did not answer directly. Instead he continued shouting, "General Aupick must be shot." I was left impressed by the lack of character which this suggested in such a refined and original person. . . .

Cited in César González-Ruano, *Baudelaire* (Madrid: Espasa-Calpe, 1958), p. 116.

Aside from lack of evidence, this statement is not convincing for several reasons. Baudelaire's working-class prose sounds at times more taken with the aesthetic consequences of the revolution than with its political benefits; he described the future race of French workers as "six feet tall and more beautiful than marble," [11] and he never spoke of 1848 with ideological nostalgia or as a man betrayed. Very soon after the revolution, and while he was still contributing to *Le Salut publique,* he was also writing for conservative journals. Eventually he dismissed 1848 in the Flaubert style as "amusing" and "charming by reason of the very excesses of its absurdity." [12]

For all the entertaining follies of modern politics, power was something to be taken seriously. The masses needed it since their instincts made them wish to be mastered. The nonmass man needed it for its own protection or for the protection of the masses against their own destructiveness. Baudelaire, who always saw the masses as a source of brute passion, said that "the real saint is he who massacres the People for the sake of the People." [13] Flaubert regarded force as so urgent a cure for modern indiscipline that he was willing to permit himself an admiration for Napoléon III. This emperor decorated photographers and exiled great poets like Victor Hugo. But he did not hesitate to use force and, for that alone, said Flaubert, "I should even go and kiss his behind." It was only unfortunate that so many people were already crowding one another to do the same, thus depriving the act of any artistic originality.[14]

But if Flaubert or Baudelaire were not conservatives in the true political sense, neither were they latter-day Machiavellians concerned with the refinements of domination as a public craft. They were not interested in the purposeful use of power, either as the implementation of a social ideology or the carrying out of the will of a constituency. The function of power for them was to surround the elite with a *cordon sanitaire* which would allow it to perform its intellectual tasks unmolested by the masses. Power also provided the artistically noble face of the political drama, just as the fiascos of utopianism provided its droll side. Baudelaire thought that "civilized" men who talked with contempt about savages and barbarians were philistines unworthy of the transports of idolatry; priests, on the other hand, were great figures because they moved the masses beyond the realm of the real and made them believe in miracles.[15] Flaubert admired the Napoleonic era because of its uncritical adoration of the Emperor, "a love exclusive, sublime, truly human." [16]

This last sentence is enough to show how deeply romantic Flaubert remained behind his efforts to be a cultural and psychological realist. It is sometimes said that the Flaubert of *Madame Bovary* is a positivist who had outgrown the romantic stereotypes of *The Temptation of St. Anthony* with its rhapsodic mixture of agony and illuminism. But this positivism is more a technique than a possession. It is a descriptive positivism, a way of collecting the elements of a social reality which he felt essentially beneath himself, while making no concessions to it. It was not a positivism of the heart. Flaubert could put together a piece of society with meticulous distaste and precision. He could also give ground and flee (as he admitted he did) to the antiquarianism of *Salammbô,* and a certain wounded aestheticism remained always a part of his outlook. Above all he never accepted the confident, discreet, manipulative body of expectations which was the core of positivism. As useful for him meant the opposite of personal so did human, in his praise of Bonapartism, mean the opposite of rational politics; in this he clearly subscribes to the opposition drawn by Stendhal between personal joy and political or industrial or bureaucratic efficiency. If the masses were to be allowed to act, they should act on some arresting impulse, some ardent belief which towered above prudence and which alone could free them from their commonplace imprisonment. Yet he realized with accusing resignation that the time for such acts was past, because the

modern masses knew nothing but utilitarian avidity and "had
lost their poetry forever." [17]

Those who would argue that there is a "sounder" and, perhaps, a more "sociological" Flaubert, could no doubt point to
his having said once that "politics will always be nonsense until it becomes a branch of science," [18] a statement which, indeed,
suggests a tough-minded interest in the possibilities of rational
action. Actually, what this remark reflects more than anything
else is Flaubert's irritation with what he regarded as the incurable and fraudulent social sanctimony of the period and,
when put in the proper context, it turns out to be one more assertion of political unconcern. "Scientific" for him was synonymous with "uncommitted"; it was the beauty of the physical
sciences, he explained, that they did not try to prove anything.
This criterion, extended to society, meant that "one must deal
with men as one does with mastodons or crocodiles." [19] Yet,
not even on the basis of this bleak analogy did he propose for
society a system of scientific observation similar to that directed
to the physical world. Such an ideal was profoundly repulsive
to him intellectually and emotionally. It was proper for the
masses to remain obedient or to glory in the worship of a heroic
figure. But to imagine a system of analysis and predictions embracing the behavior of all men was to surrender the singularity
of the elite and to destroy the element of aesthetic surprise in
historical events. No book, he wrote, not Shakespeare, nor
Goethe, nor Homer, nor the Bible, had pronounced a conclusion or rendered a verdict. Flaubert was, in his words, revolted
by the fashionable intellectual discussions of the social problem. Life was an eternal problem, as was history and everything else. A solution of the human condition would be, in the
most literal sense, a conclusion, the end.[20]

Literary alienation, in so far as it produced a social theory,
moved, then, in two directions, one moral and one artistic. The
moral strain contains a set of explanations of human behavior

which, by their very nature, exonerates the intellectual from the burden of social concern. According to Flaubert far too much attention had been paid to the so-called injustices of this world. Men would always be unjust and every flag had been soiled by blood. Socialism was nothing but another means of implementing modern mass utilitarianism and would end in nothing but institutionalized dogmatism and the obliteration of the individual. As to why the individual should be safeguarded, the answer was obvious enough. All significant values were articulate, complex, singular, and self-sanctioned. They could be understood and carried only by men who were themselves articulate, complex, and self-sanctioning. The masses had, properly speaking, not values but desires. Values, and the men who bore them, were self-demanding. The masses were self-indulgent. For this reason the creators of values and the carriers of values had it as their duty to protect themselves, to hold themselves, as it were, in trust. In former periods, society had protected the valuable individual by keeping him on the good side of aristocratic barriers. Now he must protect himself.

While the moral argument resulted in the principle of withdrawal and detachment, the artistic principle expressed the curiosity for the dramatics of human events. Like Stendhal, Flaubert and Baudelaire might have claimed that, being disillusioned enough to kill themselves at an early age, they chose to remain alive because they wondered what would happen next. In turn, this aesthetic view contributed the sense of the human predicament, a predicament whose very insolubility gave life the only meaning it possessed. Those wishing to avoid the problematic—the trapped—nature of life were counterfeiters of the human spirit. The abolitionists of Hell, Baudelaire said, would also be the abolitionists of the soul.[21] As for progress, the most persistent of the new delusions, it was the cult of the lazy and the idiotic; it was lazy because it expected "history" to do man's work, and idiotic because its actual rewards were nothing but a sop for mass gratification. Furthermore, because prog-

ress was a democratic ideal, it moved necessarily in a spiritual
void. Democratic thinking might bring an increase in public
welfare. But there was no such thing as a collective heightening
of spiritual reality. This must always be an individual act demanding a sense of problem, an introspective struggle with
meaning which cannot be performed by a body of numbers. In
other words, individual thinking was meaningful, qualitative.
Democratic thinking was always quantitative. So provoked was
the almost invariably agnostic Flaubert by what he thought the
simple-minded crassness of modern secularism that, at least
once, he allowed himself an appeal to religious mystery. Progressives and utilitarians, he cried, denied "the blood of Christ
which quickens in us." [22] Baudelaire, speaking only partly in
metaphor, exclaimed that God would never be elected by universal suffrage.[23] However, if democracy could not furnish the
spiritual basis of social order it could, through the agency of
popular education, profoundly undermine it. As Baudelaire put
it, falling once more into religious rhetoric as a means of uncovering a cultural issue, "to combat ignorance is to diminish
God." [24] In its most general sense, this is a repetition of Flaubert's appeal for human incompleteness as part of human
reality. But in a specific sense, it is Baudelaire's argument for
an intellectual aristocracy with God as a metaphor for the "divine" (art and creativity) in human experience. And it is also
an affirmation of the literary elite as a nonproselytizing clergy.
Modern educators and humanitarians constantly sought to reduce cultural distance by distributing knowledge, never realiz-
ing that they would only achieve a convivial degradation of
inherently sensitive and intricate spiritual possessions while
crowding the intellectual's breathing space in the bargain.

NOTES TO CHAPTER X

1. De Tocqueville, *Democracy in America*, **II**, 45.
2. Baudelaire, *Oeuvres complètes*, **VI**, 275; Flaubert, *Selected Letters*, p. 215.
3. Stendhal, *Mémoires d'un touriste*, **III**, 137.
4. Flaubert, *Selected Letters*, p. 209.
5. Flaubert, *Correspondance*, **II**, 117.
6. For a very helpful summary of the psychological and philosophical background from which these references are taken see J. L. Talmon, *The Rise of Totalitarian Democracy* (Boston: Beacon Press, 1952).
7. Baudelaire, *Oeuvres complètes*, **VI**, 442.
8. Flaubert, *Selected Letters*, p. 57; Steegmuller, *Flaubert and Madame Bovary*, p. 114.
9. Flottes, *op. cit.*, p. 51.
10. Plekhanov, *op. cit.*, p. 49.
11. Baudelaire, *Oeuvres complètes*, **VI**, 391-398.
12. Baudelaire, *The Essence of Laughter*, p. 178.
13. Baudelaire, *Intimate Journals*, p. 41.
14. Steegmuller, *Flaubert and Madame Bovary*, p. 249.
15. Baudelaire, *Intimate Journals*, p. 32.
16. Flaubert, *Correspondance*, **I**, 274-275.
17. Flaubert, *Selected Letters*, p. 29.
18. Flaubert, *Correspondance*, **III**, 551.
19. *Ibid.*, **II**, 236.
20. *Ibid.*, **III**, 120.
21. Baudelaire, *Oeuvres complètes*, **VI**, 278.
22. Steegmuller, *Flaubert and Madame Bovary*, p. 251.
23. Baudelaire, *Oeuvres complètes*, **VI**, 424.
24. Baudelaire, *ibid.*, **VI**, 429.

CHAPTER XI

THE LITERARY MAN IN
MODERN SOCIETY:
ALIENATION, BOREDOM,
HEDONISM, AND ESCAPE

COLIN WILSON was stating the obvious when he said that the literary outsider was, first of all, a social problem.[1] Indeed, even the name most often given to the predicament of this figure, "alienation," comes from the lexicon of psychologists and social scientists. Among these, the term has been the subject of a certain amount of professional argument, but actually some of its ordinary connotations are quite sufficient to suggest the essentials of the concept. "Alien," says Webster's dictionary, "is one who is wholly different in nature." Of course, in speaking of social alienation, no one has in mind an absolute divorce from reality or from other men, for that would be alienation in the psychiatric, not the psychological (or sociological) sense. What is meant is a sense of distance from the surroundings which represents to the person experiencing it both a burden and a necessity. The German sociologist Georg Simmel explains one of its manifestations this way:

[It] involves the somehow imagined but then rejected existence of society. Isolation attains its unequivocal significance only as society's
effect at a distance—whether as lingering of past relations, as anticipation of future contacts, as nostalgia, or as intentional turning
away from society. The isolated man does not suggest a being that
has been the only inhabitant of the globe from the beginning.[2]

The subject of these feelings is what Simmel calls the Stranger,
a figure who, in his isolation, carries within himself a longing
aftermath of social memory and the intrigue and premonition
of possible future involvement.

Like Simmel's Stranger, Baudelaire experienced his own
separation most lucidly when he was in the midst of the world
and yet hidden from the world; "multitude, solitude," he once
half exclaimed, half mused.[3] But, like Flaubert, he felt a far
more irreconcilable depth and breadth of distance. They both
spoke as men for whom social life was always an invasion of
private experience. The gulf between him and society, Baudelaire said, was a gulf "of action, dreams, memories, desires,
regrets. . . ." [4] Flaubert claimed that even as a child he had
had a forewarning of life as a "nauseous smell escaping from a
vent." [5] He once asked himself the uproarious and tragic question, "What am I doing here?",[6] meaning that some incredible,
inscrutable joke was responsible for his presence in this world.
Above all, neither wished to re-enter society or be readopted by
it. The social spectacle might kindle their curiosity, but never
so much as to cause them to surrender the sovereignty of their
apartness. To behold the world, according to Baudelaire,
was one of the pleasures of the unimpassioned and impartial
spirit, but only if the observer remained a prince who always
rejoiced in being incognito.[7]

If curiosity were one of the pleasures of the invisible observer, boredom was his constant enemy. *"Je m'ennuie,* I'm sick
to death . . . of the sickening platitude of life," wrote a
literary store clerk to a friend in 1837.[8] "I am bored," wrote
Stendhal across one of the pages of his journal as though sud-

denly overtaken by a realization which rendered all else insignificant. Flaubert, who lived with boredom as inescapable awareness—there was, he felt, neither cure nor explanation for ennui—boasted sadly that he had come into the world bored.[9] Baudelaire spoke of boredom with fear, almost as a man begging not to be seized by it, for he felt that it drove him through the despair of meaninglessness to complete irresponsibility. A bored man, he said, would willingly reduce the world to debris.[10] Boredom had, in fact, the power to produce either a reckless insensitivity or a total collapse of the capacity to retain any relation to the surroundings or even to consciousness. Using the words of a character from one of George Sand's novels, Alfred de Poittevin wondered how the restlessness of his mind could survive within the indolence of his body. He said that he felt everyday more inert, more indifferent, more paralyzed, unconscious of everything, "even of the weather." [11]

Flaubert wrote that even the most elementary physical exertions, like dressing and undressing, had become an unendurable trial.

The invisible nets of inertia that encircle my body, all the mists that float in my brain! I often feel the most killing and stupifying fatigue at the idea of having to perform the slightest action; and only with the greatest effort, sometimes, do I grasp the clearest idea. . . . It tortures me to eat, to dress, to stand on my feet. . . .[12]

Getting ready to go to a party at Destutt de Tracy's, Stendhal hoped that he would meet there "a person of exquisite breeding and absolutely no energy." [13] Powerlessness, said Baudelaire, was the god of the modern writer, and the streets and coffee houses were filled with the literary lounger, a man peculiarly combining excitability and indifference.[14]

Paralyzed as it might be by futility, the lonely literary mind could also be sustained by pride. Where nothing meant anything, the self necessarily meant all. Jean Jacques Rousseau, the first of the great modern strangers, began his *Confessions* in this way:

I was not made like anyone else I have known, perhaps, I believe, like no one else in existence. If not better I am, at least, different. If nature did well or ill to break the mold in which she formed me can only be decided after reading this book.

Whenever the last trumpet shall sound I shall appear, this book in hand, before the sovereign Judge. And I shall say loudly: "this I have done, thus I have thought, this I have been." [15]

This cult of singularity was inherited by the nineteenth century and raised by romanticism to something like the very condition of identity. Unlike the eighteenth-century political psychologists who believed in the natural partnership of all men, Stendhal simply could not conceive of another person's furnishing any part of his happiness. Baudelaire was pleased to remind himself that ("thank God") he was unlike anyone else, and for this Flaubert told him that he possessed "the highest of all virtues." [16] Actually, however, such pride of selfhood could become a heavy burden. From a purely psychological point of view we may take *The Social Contract* as a document of Rousseau's struggle to regain a sense of community by surrendering the self to the state while receiving unassailable rights in return. But for someone like Baudelaire all major discoveries seemed to be discoveries of the self at the expense of the surroundings. "What does it matter," he once remarked, "what the outside reality is made of provided that it helps me feel that I am what I am." [17] The greatest triumph of this position was the realization that a self uncommitted to the world was a self free to use the world for experience's own sake and to sample it as an exciting market place of sensations, a game for the imagination, and an opportunity for sensuous investigation. Joyfully, impudently, Flaubert made this point by offering to light up a cigar with the pages of the civil code and to exchange his civil rights for a good dinner.[18] Baudelaire's version of aesthetic fastidiousness as the companion of civic insouciance was even more elegantly amoral: "What exasperates the man of taste in the spectacle of vice," he explained, "is its deformity, its disproportion." [19]

The ecstasy of life was therefore, as Baudelaire said, the other side of the horror of life,[20] and no nineteenth-century writer was more successful in applying this principle than Stendhal. Total detachment permitted him total observation. Like Flaubert he could have said of himself, "I am an Eye." And he turned every experience, even boredom ("pure boredom . . . free from any depressing feelings"), into a discipline for cleansing away triviality and acquiring pleasurable knowledge. This capacity to keep himself in animated intellectual suspension he called "the English manner" which, coupled with "the Italian heart"—the alertness of a skilled sensitivity always allowing the beautiful to play upon the mind "like a bow" [21]—guided his great purpose of becoming a virtuoso of delectable discoveries. The reasons for going to Italy, as he outlined them in a letter to a young friend, were "sweet air, superb landscapes, love-making, fine pictures, fine churches, fine statues." [22] This is more than the incidental advice of a learned traveler. It is the life program of the perfect intellectual tourist, the observer on the loose, the man who says to life, "Here I am; please me, amuse me, intrigue me."

The notes Stendhal made on the Napoleonic invasion of Russia in 1812, during which he served as a noncombatant quartermaster officer, unveil his views with unhesitating candor. Of the fire of Smolensk, after the battle for that city, he wrote that it was "a fine spectacle" which he had stopped to watch "despite the fear of missing dinner." [23] Of Russian casualties and the terrible losses and disastrous defeats of his own compatriots he says nothing. The one thing he seems to have regretted, aside from physical discomforts, was the absence of a companionable spirit with whom to share the uncommon experiences of the campaign. This is his entry for the Moscow fire:

We left the city illuminated by the finest fire in the world. . . . It was an imposing sight, but it would have been necessary to have been alone, or else surrounded by intelligent people, in order to enjoy it. What spoiled the Italian campaign for me was to have taken part in it with people who would belittle the Colosseum or the Bay of Naples.[24]

Such statements are for Stendhal candid elucidations of his philosophy of experience, not, as we might think, supercilious shockers aimed at the reader.

But other sensitivities, more vulnerable and less fortified with Stendhal's coolness (and his somewhat mechanistic theories of sensuality) found unhappiness driving them into the refuge of art, nature, the past, or the search—actual and imaginary—for an ideal country. It was an "enervating, corruptive, brutalizing world" [25] that made Flaubert turn to an aesthetic mysticism in which he discovered, besides the terms of artistic invention, a reality capable of harboring the wounded imagination. Art, Baudelaire said, should be "a suggestive magic which contains subject and object, the external world and the artist himself." [26] Or, as we have it in his urgent dream of the *Invitation au voyage,* the movement of the mind toward a country where all was order and beauty and "even the cuisine was poetic." [27]

"Being unable to change things," wrote Émile Zola later in the century, "they [the romantics] escape into the history of dead centuries or in voyages to other countries. Theirs is the hocus pocus of legend, the local color fireworks, the immobility of the Orient and its filth, which they prefer, with their childish admiration for colorfulness, to the great accomplishments and magnificent conquests of our century of science." [28] Zola was speaking of the great tide of symbolic exile running through French literature since the romantic movement. Borel, the frustrated Caribbean Indian, also wanted to be Tahitian (a reverie later put into effect by Paul Gauguin). Flaubert, who claimed to carry within himself "the melancholy of the barbaric races, their migratory instincts, and the innate disgust with life which makes them forsake their country," wanted to be an Andalusian muleteer, a Neapolitan rogue, or, "at least the stagecoach driver between Nîmes and Marseille." [29] From literary underlings to famous authors the talk was filled with black gondolas in the night, cathedral shadows, the southern sky and, always, the East. "Alhambra," "Moorish," were shouted as words of praise at literary soirees. Flaubert, who struggled for a long time between aesthetic escape and bitter-end realism, gives us this romantic catalogue of the Oriental mirage:

The East and its vast deserts . . . its palaces trodden by camels . . . mares bounding towards the sun-flushed horizon . . . blue waves, clear sky and silvery sand . . . the smell of the warm oceans of the South; and then, near me, in a tent shaded by a broad-leaved aloe, some brown-skinned woman with burning eyes who would hold me in her arms and whisper the language of the huris.[30]

The implicit theory behind the enthusiasm and longing for the indigenous and the remote was that popular culture and "the furnace of civilization" (as Flaubert's friend de Poittevin called the scientific and utilitarian powers of which Zola was so proud) had destroyed the spontaneous relationship between daily existence and the natural aesthetic dimension of life. The search then began for societies where, as in Baudelaire's poetic cuisine, ideality and reality were one, where a customary act echoed the depths of a human truth, and where even a casual gesture was a moment of beauty. Flaubert's youthful trips in the comany of Maxime Du Camp are among the perfect examples of the theatrical and yet deadly earnest intensity of this quest. In anticipation of their journeys or during them, they did everything to leave behind their humdrum civilization and to convert themselves into colorful aborigines. To prepare themselves to go to Brittany in 1847, they acquired white hats from Avignon, Tyrolese pipes, and Hungarian tobacco pouches. In Egypt, they adopted the Moslem costume. In Athens, they dressed in Near Eastern style and bowed before the Greek queen with a "Turkish salute" as she processionally went by.

Naturally, this was all quite vicarious and Flaubert's occasional talk of becoming a Moslem must be taken as only another metaphor of displeasure. He could not have accepted another world any more than he could have adopted his own, and if he ever had envisioned an ideal society, it would be one in which "one is not obliged to be a citizen . . . to vote, to be a member of a jury." [31] For the real issue was an uprootedness which no fantasy could lay to rest. While Flaubert was in the Orient he longed for his home province of Normandy, and he tells the story of one of his friends who spent the years of his stay in Calcutta poring over a map of Paris only to do the same with a map of Calcutta after returning to Paris. [32]

Yet the phenomenon of exoticism is significant, and it has left its mark in art, literature, anthropology, and the psychology of modern travel. For the alienated individual, the cultivation of cultural remoteness represented the entrance into a symbolic community to which he gave the fullness of intellectual loyalty without having to meet any demands for actual adjustment. There were three reasons for this. Remote societies were regarded as undivided and having a natural wholeness; thus intellectual membership in them was a comfortable thing which relieved the tension caused by actual social isolation (Zola was right about the literary preference for the "immobility" of faraway civilizations, though perhaps he did not understand its sources). Motivations in such societies were thought to come from nonutilitarian impulses, and entire cultures were thought to have the same aesthetic integrity which the literary man attributed to himself. In Brittany, Flaubert marveled at the primitive's instinct for emotional grandeur while watching a fisherman's wife weep over the body of her husband washed ashore by the sea. From Egypt, he wrote about the elegance of the natives' expressions and stances. In the case of nomads he assumed that they moved because, like himself, they were afflicted with *Weltschmerz*. Finally, being whole and "inspired," these cultures were also unique, which meant that intellectuals could identify themselves with them without surrendering their personal originality.

Next to the companionship of idealized societies was the companionship of idealized nature. The worlds of commerce and technology were numerical and mechanistic. Nature was spontaneously orderly and spontaneously creative, and contact with it restored in man that sense of living completeness which had been tarnished and starved by money, machines, and the narrow rationalistic demands of modern civilization. Nature was an undemanding source of vital fulfillment, an embrace both free and protective. In short, it made possible spiritually meaningful solitude. Inevitably, because of the emotions it aroused, nature-contemplation became a widespread item of literary alienation. It was not, however, a universal attitude. Stendhal, who grew up through the height of romanticism, was essentially unaffected by it. He cultivated the appreciation of the landscape as part of the repertory of an educated taste, but nothing could have been more foreign to him than the romantic notion of a dialogue between Nature and Man. Flaubert, on the other hand, turned to nature for the same kind of consolation he had sought in antiquity and exotic folkways.

My own passion for it [nature] is becoming uncontrollable. At times I look at animals and even at trees with a tenderness that amounts to a feeling of affinity; I derive almost voluptuous sensations from just seeing.[33]

Baudelaire represents, in this case, a mild puzzle. He was deeply inclined to a nonrational view of the person and of human purpose, and endowed his language with echoes of religious implications pointing to the glowing mystery and tragic character of human experience. He cursed tools and utensils in the name of God as he feared for God at the hands of technology. But he refused to seek the embrace of nature, and remained thoroughly urban all his life. The answer to this seeming discrepancy may be found in the fundamental ambivalence toward the city which he shared with other writers. The city was the setting of the things he dreaded most—the factory, the merchants, and the mob—and he despised its politics and its economics. But he loved its freedom, and its opportunities for anonymity and curious observation.

There is in Baudelaire, however, a theme which provides the link between intellectual withdrawal and the vision of nature as the friend and protector of the isolated man. A poet, he writes, should always avoid those places where "the rich and the joyous congregate," and he should feel drawn to everything "feeble, destitute, orphaned, and forlorn." [34] This meant, of course, that the poet should be willing to concede impotence, because, in a world where victory went to materialistic efficiency, failure is to be honored as spiritual excellence. This idea joins another admirable form of unsuccess or, rather, anti-success—the admiration of ruins. There is in Western culture an old tradition of poetic contemplation of ruins which, in revealing the temporariness of things, leaves the onlooker thoughtfully nostalgic, chastened, and wiser. For the haters of modern culture, ruins were more than that. What they saw in ruins was the work of nature as the avenger of the sensitive but powerless person in the face of technological arrogance. Men who could not control the environment could always hope that a force larger than they would achieve the destruction of the things which society had built and teach society that there was yet a greater truth than materialistic dreams and the empire of tools.

The ore is homesick. And it wants to foresake the coins and the wheels which teach it a petty way of living. And out of the factories and out of the money chests, it will return into the veins of the gaping holes which will clamp shut behind it.[35]

The message of these lines by Rainer Maria Rilke is perfectly plain. Usefulness is a diminution, a fragmentation, a cutting and chiseling at a living thing for the sake of the momentary and the superficial. The return of the ore to the vein is a victory of a total, living, and sacred reality over a pedestrian and opportunistic exploitation of the sacred; it is a victory of being over doing and making. Not long ago, after a visit to New York, the Spanish poet García Lorca prophesied that the Stock Exchange would in time be a pyramid of moss, and that cobras would some day hiss in the upper stories of skyscrapers.[36] In his own day Flaubert wrote:

I love above all the sight of vegetation resting upon old ruins; this embrace of nature coming swiftly to bury the work of man the moment that his hand is no longer there to defend it, fills me with deep joy.[37]

NOTES TO CHAPTER XI

1. Colin Wilson, *The Outsider* (Boston: Houghton Mifflin Co., 1956), p. 11.

2. Georg Simmel, *The Sociology of Georg Simmel*, ed. & trans. Kurt H. Wolff (Glencoe, Ill.: The Free Press, 1950), p. 119.

3. Baudelaire, *The Essence of Laughter*, p. 139.

4. Cited in Sartre, *op. cit.*, p. 41.

5. Cited in Martin Turnell, *The Novel in France* (New York: Vintage Books, 1958), p. 263.

6. Flaubert, *Correspondance*, **I**, 28.

7. Baudelaire, *The Essence of Laughter*, p. 29.

8. Cited in Maigron, *op. cit.*, p. 30.

9. Spencer, *op. cit.*, p. 22.

10. Bennett, *op. cit.*, p. 39.

11. Steegmuller, *Flaubert and Madame Bovary*, p. 30.

12. Cited in *ibid.*, p. 213.

13. Stendhal, *Memoirs of Egotism*, p. 161.

14. Baudelaire, *Oeuvres complètes*, **VI**, 48.

15. Jean Jacques Rousseau, *Confessions* (Geneva: 1782), pp. 1-2.

16. Bennett, *op. cit.*, p. 9; Flaubert, *Selected Letters*, p. 197.

17. Cited in Sartre, *op. cit.*, p. 22.

18. Flaubert, *Correspondance*, **I**, 89.

19. Cited in Bennett, *op. cit.*, p. 56.

20. Sartre, *op. cit.*, p. 76.

21. Stendhal, *Private Diaries*, p. 395.

22. Stendhal, *To the Happy Few*, p. 246.

23. *Ibid.*, p. 137.

24. Stendhal, *Private Diaries*, p. 483.

25. Cited in Steegmuller, *op. cit.*, p. 250.

26. Cited in Sartre, *op. cit.*, pp. 22-23.

27. Baudelaire, *Oeuvres complètes,* **III**, 51.

28. Cited in Maigron: *op. cit.*, p. 10.

29. Cited in Emile Faguet, *Flaubert* (London: Constable & Co., 1914), p. 30.

30. Cited in Spencer, *op. cit.,* 38.

31. Flaubert, *Correspondance,* **IV**, 38.

32. Spencer, *op. cit.*, p. 72.

33. Flaubert, *Selected Letters,* p. 36.

34. Baudelaire, *Paris Spleen* (New York: New Directions, 1947), p. 22.

35. Cited in Peter Viereck, "The Poet in the Machine Age," *Journal of the History of Ideas,* **I**, No. 1, January, 1949, p. 98.

36. Federico García Lorca, *El Poeta en Nueva York* (Mexico: Editorial Seneca, 1940), p. 58.

37. Flaubert, *Corespondance,* **I**, 224.

CHAPTER XII

THE LITERARY MAN IN
MODERN SOCIETY:
A PECULIAR ARISTOCRACY

ON MARCH 26, 1847, Prime Minister Guizot arose on the floor
of the Chamber of Deputies to speak against an amendment to
the electoral law which proposed to give the vote to persons of
intellectual distinction without regard for property or income.
The electoral system of France, Guizot said, did not conceive
the vote as the momentary act of an individual. It was rather
the expression of the social interests and relations of the voter
and of the bonds uniting him with those social groups which had
a natural title to parliamentary representation. The amendment
would grant political rights to intellectuals without taking into
account their social station and would, in effect, recognize intelligence as a social rank in itself. To this Guizot objected as
follows:

Gentlemen, I have infinite respect for intelligence; it is one of the
virtues, and it will be one of the titles of honor of our time to have
high respect for knowledge and to give it its due. But I myself do not
blindly trust intelligence nor do I believe that others should have

such trust, least of all in our time. Excessive confidence in human intelligence, human pride, intellectual pride—let us call things by their names—these things are the disease, the cause of a large part of our errors and our evils. Intelligence, as I have had the honor to say in this chamber so frequently, must at all times be guarded, restrained, guided by social conditions. The proponents of the amendment treat modern intelligence as one treated in former days the aristocracy. It seems that one should demand of intelligence that it should be noble and that it be nothing else. . . .[1]

Guizot was genuinely of two minds on the question of the public place of intellectuals. He liked to think of himself as one. He conceded that the intellectual monopoly of the Church had been ended. He was both impressed and disturbed by the "brilliance" of the new "moral" (that is, social) sciences. And all of these things were undoubtedly in his thoughts when he spoke in 1847.[2] But the speech is also the document of a general dilemma. In his praiseful asides on the dignity of the life of the minds, and in his reminder to the Chamber of the many times he had debated the point, Guizot reveals to what extent the status of the intellectual had become a social issue in Orleanist France, just as his reasons for rejecting the electoral amendment voices the response of the ruling class to the intellectuals' contention that their work was inherently well-deserving. The price of political recognition Guizot suggested was rather a dutiful attachment to the social order. This, however, led to a problem of spiritual management: how to administer the test of rectitude to writers without turning literature into some sort of public "service." *

* Alexandre Dumas (*père*) gives the following appraisal of Guizot and of his relations with intellectuals:

> M. Guizot . . . a studious, grave man, rigidly puritanical (Guizot was a Protestant), put into practice in the Chamber of Deputies in 1830 the same social ideas he had ripened during his tenure in the Chamber of Peers. Dedicated intellectually to a system and not sentimentally to a dynasty, he did not yield too readily to artistic courtliness. Rather he instinctively . . . turned to the philologist, the historian, the savant, and extended his patronage only to university profes-

There were two kinds of literature, "national" and "individual."
The first required a form of mass solidarity based on a common
fund of ideas which no longer existed in modern society. The
second could only be sustained by intellectual diversity. Flaubert looked at national literature in the same way that the romantics looked at national history, as the expression of a unique
spiritual collectivity. In a national literature the problem of freedom did not really exist. There was no opposition between the
work of art and cultural reality because national life was a human architecture radiating a unified inner principle which had
in itself the characteristics of a work of art. On the other hand,
individual literature, the only literature possible in a noncul-
tural world such as the present one could, for obvious reasons,
exist only by the privileges of tolerance and difference.[3]

Yet, how was creative freedom to exist in a society so jeal-
ously dedicated to the commonplace? This question, which embraced both the struggle for self-justification and the covert
need for an audience (all literary work must, somehow, be a
gesture of communication), was answered in a number of passionate ways. With a fear which was the other side of their
profound loathing for the middle class, Flaubert and Baudelaire
sometimes spoke of merchants who amused themselves by
"roasting" poets and of writers and artists as a new race of
gladiators whose mission it was to entertain the public with their
"agonies." [4] Politically impotent and still firm in their sense of
superiority, they retreated at other times into fantasies which
conferred upon them not only respect and leadership, but unlimited power. Baudelaire liked to imagine himself as one of the

---

sors, the compilers of chronicles, the decipherers of charts.
Any work outside such austere literature seemed to him
unworthy of support and encouragement. As a result the
works of *esprit*, of imagination, of poetry, were thrown on
their own resources, left painfully to find their way. . . .

Alexandre Dumas, *Souvenirs dramatiques* (2 vols.; Paris: Michel Levy
Frères, 1868), I, 181.

warring popes of the Renaissance, a dream which blended his admiration for the mystical and military forms of authority.[5] Flaubert wandered back to pagan hero-worship and smelled "the frankincense burning around the chariot of the conqueror." [6] He felt he had been born to be Emperor of Cochin China, to smoke pipes fifty yards long, have a thousand wives, ride Numidian mares, and take his ease by marble fountains. (In order to please the aesthetic imagination, power had to be not only absolute but also magnificently decorative.)[7] More abstractly he would say that he despised modern tyranny because it was weak and fearful of itself, but that he had a deep reverence for ancient tyranny "as the most beautiful manifestation of mankind." [8] The contention that ancient tyranny, by being absolute, was not only efficient but beautiful, is nothing if not a symptom of the artistic individualist's frustrated enthusiasm for power. Absolutism, as Flaubert admired it, ruled over a glittering and arresting sweep of events wholly unlike the workaday performance of ordinary social services. Like art itself, tyranny was personal, not only as a public expression, but as an expression, extension, and refinement of individual conduct which allowed for drama, splendor, and the heroic. One could say of Flaubert's tyrant what Valéry said of Stendhal: for him life was a private stage upon which he presented without interruption the performance of himself.[9]

Oddly enough, it was the tireless artist of egotism, Stendhal, who in this respect entertained something more than exciting personal dreams. He was, of the three, the closest to rationalism —his psychology, in fact, reads like an aesthetic rendition of eighteenth-century mechanistic mentalism à la Holbach—and the one freest of romantic notions about intellectual ineffability. For that reason, perhaps, Stendhal was willing to embrace within the elite, not only writers, but academicians, lawyers, doctors, and architects. He proposed also to give such persons institutional recognition by opening to them as many parliamentary seats as the electoral law accorded the merchants of Mar-

seille, Lyons, and Bordeaux and by the establishment of a college of peers, which would place the young aristocracy under
the tutelage of cultivated men. The prospective students at this
institution—a kind of finishing school for civil servants—would
be boys between fourteen and nineteen from upper-class families who would work their way through a curriculum not unlike
the "great books" and "great issues" courses of our day. The required reading list would include de Tracy, Say, Montesquieu,
Helvetius, Gibbon, and Machiavelli, besides keeping abreast of
the daily press and parliamentary record and attending parliamentary debates. Stendhal thought also that intellectuals
should serve as arbiters between contending social classes.[10]

Dubious in its applicability as this scheme sounds (it appears, one should add, as an incidental speculation in the midst
of a variety of other notes), it was still a pragmatically intended view of intellectual leadership. Flaubert's ideas on the
other hand were more general and more imperious, and curiously resemble the medieval theory of *saniors pars,* the sounder
part, as opposed to the verdicts of the quantitative majority.
Popular suffrage as the moral and legal foundation of the public
order he thought, of course, an amazing jest of which society
itself was the butt. His own proposal for the new legitimacy was
a majority of "something more than numbers," the rule of "God's
own aristocracy" (*l'aristocratie du bon Dieu*).[11] Among the
"mandarins" who would constitute it (this expression, now
fashionable, is Flaubert's own) he listed, besides literary artists,
scholars like Renan and scientists like Littré, which is somewhat
surprising since Flaubert, like Baudelaire, tended to think of
the intellectual elite as composed of men whose pecularity was
social and spiritual and not based on mere intellectual accom-
plishment. Baudelaire, as we remember, banished from his
aristocracy all those engaged in professional duties. He also
stigmatized social thinkers as platitudinous do-gooders, as he
did anti-clericalists, perhaps because the anti-religiousness of the
latter reflected a vulgar narrowness of the imagination. But if

Flaubert was willing to take in a scholar or two, he kept out humanitarians (a "dreary race") and all organized forms of intellect. Professors he regarded as bureaucratized pedants whom he wanted to "wrap all into one package and chuck . . . down the toilet." On philosophy his comment was, "merde." [12]

How a species apart like the mandarins ("a monstrosity, something outside of nature") would exercise its domination, Flaubert did not say, as, indeed, he could not say. Like the democrats and progressives he excoriated, he too was, in his own way, an utopian for whom perfection alone could reclaim the alienated sensitivity. He was thus condemned to be always on the outside and always "right." "The day I stop being indignant," he said, "I'll have nothing left to live for." There was no choice for him but to retreat behind an inaccessible and spiteful impassivity.

It is well nowadays to keep to oneself and leave that sort of thing [democratic aspirations] to the rabble, who are always pushing themselves forward and crowding the public places. As for us, let us stay home: from our balcony let us watch the public go by, and if at times we're too bored, then let's spit on their heads and continue to talk quietly and watch the sun sink below the horizon.[13]

This principle of withdrawal could even lead to the wish for intellectual self-annihilation as a means of delivery from society. Though he was not a purveyor of brooding ambivalences in the romantic fashion, Flaubert felt sometimes that the creative "monster" could use its intellectual powers to get rid of itself, cornered as it was by isolation. This seems to be the psychological meaning of the naturalistic doctrines of his later life, which battled for a literary discipline so perfect in its capacity to embrace and reveal the world, that the artist would disappear within the reality of its own creation. "Art has nothing to do with the artist," he said; "he must manage to lead posterity to believe that he did not exist at all." [14] Baudelaire expressed the same wish for vanishment by allowing the senses to dissolve into a drifting aesthetic dream.

Come then, what do you love, odd one, stranger? I love clouds . . .
the passing clouds.[15]

Even the *épatant* game of literary provocation could become a
means of inviting destruction, causing society to expose itself in
its vindictive crassness, and the artist in his suicidal spiritual
self-esteem. After finishing *Salammbô,* Flaubert wrote:

It will: 1) annoy the bourgeois . . . ; 2) unnerve and shock sensitive people; 3) anger the archeologists; 4) be unintelligible to the
ladies; 5) earn me a reputation as a pederast and a cannibal. Let us
hope so.[16]

This leads us to that mixture of social accusation and self-
justifying need to be among the outcast which is an inseparable
part of modern literary suffering. Fatherlessness and illegiti-
macy were among the most literal ideals of romantic writing.
F. W. Draper has counted something like thirteen orphans and
bastards in a handful of romantic plays, and one of the young
literary aspirants studied by Maigron wrote, disarmingly invok-
ing the price of the creative "curse": "I would give half my
talents to be a bastard. What a beautiful play I would *then*
write . . ." (my italics).[17] Baudelaire was not so confident
about the productive effects of the "curse." He boasted of it, of
course, hoping that idiots and maniacs might be found among
his ancestors and recalling de Vigny's saying that the poet had
"a malediction upon his life and a blessing upon his name." [18]
But self-awareness and the taste of what D. H. Lawrence
would later call a world "tainted with oneself" [19] could also revolt and exhaust him. At such moments the Stranger would fall
from his lyrical reverie to become a "cloud-monger" and a
"damned bastard." Still, one more weapon was left. A deeper
rebellion which turned ultimate self-accusation into ultimate
self-assertion—the pride of self-hatred. "When I shall have inspired universal horror," he said, "I shall have conquered solitude." [20]

Baudelaire recognized that there were ways of escaping from

society, such as drugs, which permitted a variety of opportunities for illusion to the artist's insatiable self (both the teeming religiosity, and the mystical attachment to the transcendence of drug experience in the present-day Bohemians of Mailer and Kerouac is traceable to nineteenth-century romanticism and its aftermath. In an essay on the effects of hashish written in 1851, Baudelaire speaks of the boundless fluidity of sense and imagination created by it; of the torrential associations of words, the transformation of sounds into colors, colors into music, and music into numbers; of the rhapsodic suggestiveness of the smallest noise; and, above all, of the "hurricane of pride" which leads the mind "to that glittering abyss in which it will gaze upon the face of Narcissus."

A wild and ardent shout breaks forth from his bosom with such force, such projectile power, that if the wishes of a drunken man had any effective virtue, the shout would bowl over the angels scattered on the paths of Heaven: "I am God." [21]

In *The Poem of Hashish,* Baudelaire documented the faculty of drugs to give a "lost" soul a moment of "holiness," and to break "the heavy darkness of communal and day-to-day existence"; "laying on of hands," he said, was not too strong a description of such an experience. But there was also remorse in it, a remorse somewhat theatrical and voluptuously confessional, yet containing a plausible note of fear and a sense that the drug-induced utopia was too ravished and too ephemeral to give literary artists the bearing, the assurance, even the mask which Baudelaire thought they needed. Nor would self-hatred do it, for all the temptations of its reverse narcissism.

What was needed was a turning of the artist's susceptibility inside out, a marshaling of everything that made him vulnerable —sensitivity, imagination, nonsecularity—into a self-proclaimed discipline of severely cultivated refinement.

The means to achieve this began first with a transformation of the artist's outward appearance. Attempts by people to effect an unusual appearance, says George Plekhanov, should be

the subject of sociological studies because they are a reflection
of the social relations of a period.[22] The history of such efforts
among intellectuals is part of the history of their struggle with
their social surroundings. In the early 1900's, Clovis Hugues,
poet and member of the French Chamber of Deputies, maintained that to trim one's hair was a dangerous concession to the
bourgeoisie.[23] Earlier, when Tennyson was to be seated in the
House of Lords, he had to be dissuaded by his friends from
wearing his poet's hat to the ceremony.[24] Stefan George in Germany, Henri Bergson in France, Miguel de Unamuno in Spain
all wore the clerical collar in obedience to the doctrine of the
sacerdoce littéraire. This doctrine, like the tradition of "artistic"
dressing still present in the capes, cravats, and chevelures of
orchestra conductors, philosophers, painters, and great architects, comes to us from the romantic movement and, together
with these well-established (and publicized) idiosyncrasies, is
part of a characteristically modern effort to turn intellectual
experience into a social style.

Some of the appurtenances of this way of life can be found in
the leisure of Stendhal's "English manner," in the wisdom of
the senses of "Italian heart," and, more particularly, in another
device of personal stylistics which he called his "Spanish sentiments." Romanticism had been responsible for a Spanish fad in
French letters which combined the long-standing tradition of
Spanish pride with an idealization of Spain as one of those
countries not yet contaminated by the commercialism and rationalism of modern life. For instance, a prototype of Hugoist
heroics like the protagonist of *Hernani,* a bandit of obscure (but
actually royal) birth, fearfully impulsive and infinitely proud,
filled the measure of romantic excellence by being also a Span-
iard. Actually, however, the essential ingredient of Stendhal's
Spanish feelings is not exotic bravado but an intellectualized
expression of traditional honor manifested in two ways: an
aristocratic helplessness before practical matters which, Stendhal was pleased to admit, made him the natural prey of huck-

sters and merchants and an avoidance, through the "mad aloneness" of the Spanish character, of the "ugly collection of details" which constituted the world of bourgeois affairs.[25]

From Stendhal's impeccable unsecularity we may step to an even more dedicated, artful, and desperate gesture dealing with the problem of literary estrangement. This consisted in the ritual organization of the writer's appearance and personal and intellectual manner in a way which turned him into a public minority, a caste. Since the artist was essentially powerless before society, he would then be compelled through self-exposure to attain the only form of control and pride available to him: self-pride and self-control. Such was the scheme, dream, and ordeal designed to convert the literary man into a regal outcast contained in Baudelaire's theory of the Dandy. Baudelaire evolved this figure, at least in part, and not as oddly as we might imagine, from his intellectual admiration of the world of cats. Bertrand Russell remarks that romantics, having always put beauty ahead of utility, preferred tigers to worms. Darwin, a scientist and not a romantic, preferred the worm. Blake, a poet and a romantic, preferred the tiger.[26] Baudelaire, who had a romantic's repugnance for homely and dutiful exertions but also a sensuous, though calculated, sense of form, gave his praises to cats because they appeared to him as the very embodiment of well-managed voluptuousness and luxurious self-involvement. In his own version of the relation between the physical and the spiritual Baudelaire suggested the cat's virtues, "the cult of oneself as the lover of oneself" as the goal of the Dandy. He added, so that there would be no doubt about the meaning of his symbol as a guide for the intellectual aristocracy, that the rabble and people of democratic tendencies always hated cats.[27]

Although the Dandy was intended to be much more than a mere fop, Baudelaire himself recognized a certain kinship between the two types as systems of significant affectation or, as he put it, of a "rigorously artificial code of behavior." [28] We may

find a bridge between the two in Barbey d'Aurevilly, who, like
Flaubert, had become disturbed by the destruction of social
distinctions through the uniformity of fashion. An entry in
d'Aurevilly's diary tells us how he spent hours choosing the precise coat and trousers appropriate to the events of the day,
a matter "grave . . . almost religious," as he said, with a
straight-faced exaggeration which conveyed his concern that
intellectuals should develop a form of attire equal to their
singular position in society.[29] Baudelaire looked on this issue in
the same spirit of conscientiously petulant observance, as this
contemporary description shows.

Slowly, with a slightly swaying, slightly feminine gait, Baudelaire
crossed the avenue of trees at the Porte de Namur. He was meticulously careful to avoid the mud, and if it was raining, hopped on the
pointed toes of his pumps in which he liked to look at his reflection.
He was freshly shaven with his hair combed back in a bunch behind
his ears. He wore a soft collar of snowy white which could be seen
above the collar of his cloak and which made him look like a clergy-
man or an actor.[30]

Yet, as with all symbols which are both apparent realities
and mirrors of the indwelling, this finely-staged deportment was
only the visible side of the spiritual profile of the Dandy which
Baudelaire draws as follows:

> A great man and a saint, for his own sake.
> Lives and sleeps in front of a mirror
> Is a man of leisure and general
>   education
> Is rich and loves work
> Works in a disinterested manner
> Does nothing useful
> Is either a poet, a priest, or a soldier
> Is solitary
> Is unhappy
> Never speaks to the masses except to insult
>   them
> Never touches a newspaper.[31]

What characterized the Dandy, then, were certain peculiar forms of intellectual suffering and certain singular intellectual duties. Through the sainthood of self-adoration Baudelaire sought to give the Dandy something like a heroic character and a training method for those who chose distress because of self-imposed demands. For suffering was not only the lot of the Dandy but a need and, in some ways, a right. It was the philosophical justification of egocentrism, and it taught that, in a culturally debauched society, such egocentrism represented no indulgence but rather the struggle for high values. It stood, therefore, both as a spiritual cross and a spiritual ornament. "You are a happy man," Baudelaire wrote to Jules Janin, "I am sorry for you, and I feel that my ill humor is more distinguished than your bliss." [32] The occupations and interests of the Dandy were either traditionally transcendental—art, war, and the divine—or aesthetic manipulations of the otherwise prosaic medium of money. Like Frédéric Amiel, Baudelaire believed that "high life" was a form of poetry and remarked that all French writers of upper-class novels had always judiciously provided their characters with financial substance so that they might devote themselves to the unobstructed pursuit of fantasy. Money, used in the interest of sensitivity, made it possible to translate reverie into reality and to purchase the time-freedom without which eroticism would be not art but vulgar pleasure or, worse still, marital life and, consequently, social and "repugnantly useful" duty.[33]

Baudelaire insisted, however, that the first obligation of the Dandy was, not to immoderate material elegance, but to the avoidance of excess. On this issue the grounds of Dandyism begin to shift from a concern with the conditions of cultivated inactivity to a description of the precise content and boundaries of the Dandy's intellectual stand and personal demeanor. Baudelaire asks himself, "What is the passion which, having become doctrine . . . is capable of forming such a haughty caste." And his answer is:

[A]bove all, the ardent desire to create an originality contained within the outward limits of propriety. . . . It is the pleasure of astonishing and the proud satisfaction of never having been astonished oneself. A Dandy may be blasé, he may suffer, but, in the latter case, he will smile like the Spartan when bitten by the fox.[34]

The Dandy was to be a *caste provoquante* representing "what is best in human pride, the need, rare today, to combat and destroy triviality," and he suggested "for the priests and victims of this strange spiritualism" an impeccable attire which would announce their lofty standards and the practice of dangerous sports to fortify them in their daily tasks.[35] Reading such proposals today we may think ourselves before an uncomfortable bit of posturing, but Baudelaire took Dandyism quite seriously as a new kind of monasticism which, like the monasteries of the Dark Ages, would shelter values in a time of cultural destruction. It represented for him the spiritual exclusivism of the cultural *declassé* in a democratic age, the last (and wholly intellectual) glimmer of the aristocratic tradition before it was overtaken by spiritually pre-empted equalitarianism.

In such troubled times some men repelled, jobless, taskless, but rich in native power, come to conceive the foundations of a new sort of aristocracy, one which will be especially difficult to destroy because it is founded upon the most precious and most indestructible of endowments, and upon the heavenly gifts which neither labor nor money can confer.[36]

The Dandy's intention, then, was to defy society with the perfection of the individual. To bolster and to nurture everything that marked the borderline between the indiscriminate "others" and the supremely well-sculptured ego of the aesthete. In this unyielding singularity as well as in his worshipful attitude toward art, the Dandy may be called a descendant of the Bohemian. He may, in fact, be called a super-Bohemian who leaves the turbulence of the early days and replaces it with a newly gained composure. It is in the failure to recognize the possibility of this later style that one finds the principal weakness of certain academic discussions of the Bohemian personality. This is the case, for instance, with the theories of W. I. Thomas and Florian Znaniecki, familiar to every American student of sociology. According to these writers there are three basic human types—the philistine, the creative, and the Bohemian— whose peculiarities of behavior depend on different measures of temperament and character. Temperament is a group of unco-ordinated but original personal attitudes independent of social influence. Character is a set of attitudes developed by social influence. Temperament is instinctive, character reflective. The reflective attitudes of the philistine are directed only to the most predictable, safest, and most expedient social goals. The creative person combines willingness to experiment with a capability to plan. The Bohemian is ruled by a swirl of socially unrelated dispositions and never develops a scheme of life. He is, in other words, the prototype of the characterless person.[37]

Now, aside from the scientific validity of such concepts as instinctive attitude, it is obvious that this theory does not fit literary Bohemianism, elitism, or Dandyism, even as a mere description. One could say that these intellectual postures exhibit no character, no "scheme of life," only if one accepts the indirectly moralistic leanings of the theories of Thomas and Znaniecki. For them, character refers always by implication to respectable patterns of adjustment to the society as a whole. But Dandyism, while not a pattern of adjustment, is, most emphatically, even obsessively, a plan, a program of life. What gives it its peculiar quality and, indeed, its significance as a sociological phenomenon, is just the fact that it constitutes a personality *tour de force* aimed at organizing all of life within a system of values that is completely individualistic and, at the same time, coherent. Characterlessness, in the Thomas and Znaniecki account, derives from a disorganization of attitudes and a lack of intellectual purpose. But the Dandy is the very opposite of all this, for his very separation from society depends on the most delicate and self-conscious organization of intellectual attitudes. One may say, in fact, that the Dandy has nothing but character.

This, then, takes us to the reversal of self-disappearance and into the absolute self-assertion and self-exhibition as the only answer to the distance between the artist and the public. In the beginning of its history *la vie de Bohème* had been nearly inseparable from the romantic ideals of personality and art. The Dandy represents an effort to disengage the Bohemian from the romantic. Baudelaire disliked the storminess and high-flung spontaneity of the romantics, their wish to be "natural" and to let every emotion take its course. Nevertheless, he admired the Bohemian spirit because it was moved by a desire to create a code of gestures and manner marking off the man of letters as a separate being. Théophile Gautier, who was one of the most readily dithyrambic celebrants of *l'art pour l'art,* gave this description of Baudelaire in which the poet becomes the monument of his own ideal:

His gestures were slow, sober and rare; for he held Southern gesticulation in horror. Neither did he like volubility of speech, and British reserve appealed to his sense of good form. One might describe him as a dandy strayed into Bohemia; but preserving his rank and that cult of oneself which characterizes a man imbued with the principles of Brummel. . . . His appearance was striking; he had closely shaved hair of rich black, over a forehead of extraordinary whiteness, giving his head the appearance of a Saracen helmet. His eyes colored like tobacco of Spain, had great depth and spirituality about them, and a certain penetration which was, perhaps, a little too insistent. As to the mouth, in which the teeth were white and perfect, it was seen under a slight and silky mustache which screened its contours. The mobile curves, voluptuous and ironical as the lips in a face painted by Leonardo da Vinci, the nose fine and delicate, somewhat curved, with quivering nostrils, seemed ever to be scenting vague perfumes. . . .[38]

One can hardly escape in such painted-silk prose the impact of the teacher upon the disciple, and all of it may appear to us

today, distressingly, as tortuously exhibitionistic. But for Baudelaire, this was nothing but the dream of arming the literary
rebel with carriage and poise. His hope led him from youthful
and undisciplined origins to maturity and invincible self-
confidence to create a spiritual version of the gentleman and
to elevate it to monastic precision. The human model thus
brought into existence would encompass intellectual splendor,
arrogance, and restraint—what he called "the majestic modesty" of the man of letters.

NOTES TO CHAPTER XII

1. François Guizot, *Histoire parlementaire de France* (5 vols.; Paris:
1861), V, 385-386.

2. Guizot, *Mémoires*, I, 227.

3. Flaubert, *Correspondance*, II, 44.

4. Flaubert, *Selected Letters*, p. 202; Baudelaire, *Intimate Journals*,
p. 47.

5. Sartre, *op. cit.*, p. 156.

6. Flaubert, *Selected Letters*, p. 44.

7. Spencer, *op. cit.*, p. 46.

8. Flaubert, *Selected Letters*, p. 57.

9. Turnell, *op. cit.*, p. 135.

10. Stendhal, *Mélanges de politique et d'histoire*, pp. 84f., 226.

11. Flaubert, *Correspondance*, II, 109.

12. *Ibid.*, II, 109; I, 60.

13. Flaubert, *Selected Letters*, pp. 21-22.

14. Cited in Faguet, *op. cit.*, pp. 42-43.

15. Baudelaire, *Oeuvres complètes*, III, 11.

16. Cited in Spencer, *op. cit.*, p. 160.

17. Cited in Maigron, *op. cit.*, p. 104.

18. Cited in Flottes, *op. cit.*, p. 44.

19. D. H. Lawrence, *Selected Poems* (New York: New Directions,
1947), p. 75.

20. Baudelaire, *Intimate Journals*, p. 22.

21. Baudelaire, *The Essence of Laughter*, p. 101.

22. Plekhanov, *op. cit.*, p. 46.

23. Alvin Frances Sanborn, *Paris and the Social Revolution* (Boston:
Small Maynard and Co.), p. 213.

24. Schücking, *op. cit.,* p. 21.

25. Stendhal, *The Life of Henri Brulard,* pp. 167, 169.

26. Bertrand Russell, *A History of Western Philosophy,* p. 678.

27. Baudelaire, *Intimate Journals,* p. 49; Flottes, *op. cit.,* p. 97.

28. Cited in Bennett, *op. cit.,* p. 39.

29. Starkie, *op. cit.,* p. 82.

30. Cited in Sartre, *op. cit.,* p. 148.

31. Baudelaire, *Oeuvres complètes,* **VI,** 95.

32. Cited in Sartre, *op. cit.,* p. 148.

33. Baudelaire, *Oeuvres complètes,* **IV,** 241.

34. *Ibid.,* **IV,** 241-242.

35. *Ibid.,* **IV,** 243.

36. *Loc. cit.*

37. William I. Thomas & Florian Znaniecki, *The Polish Peasant in Europe and America* (3 vols.; Boston: The Gorham Press, 1919), **III,** 18.

38. Théophile Gautier, *His Life* (London: Greening & Co., 1915), pp. 2, 62.

Part 3
The Heritage of Alienation: Productivity, Social Efficiency, and Intellectual Gloom

ONE OF THE DOMINANT features of the nineteenth century was
a profoundly disturbed intellectual life. Another, however, was
the triumph of the idea of progress and the rousing spectacle
of economic and scientific achievements which for many men
confirmed the power and the truth of this new faith. The same
historical period that gave rise to most of our present traditions
of literary anger and injury invented the industrial exposition
with its pageantry of material conquest, its ceremonials of
technological pride, and its historical message that in the new
society the economic function was no longer a backstage
chore relegated to classes which, since Plato, had been regarded
as morally tainted by virtue of their very usefulness and efficiency. Indeed, one may say that the nineteenth century turned
Francis Bacon's philosophical slogan, "knowledge is power,"
into a social reality, because science, which shared with business so much of the modern approval, owed a great deal of its
own repute to the services which it could render to business.

These two great forces, business and technology, affected not only the material aspects of modern life but the most basic cultural perspectives of social worth. The unprecedented skills which they demanded and created for the mastery of the natural environment, as well as the techniques of production, transportation, and distribution of goods they caused to develop, were both so complex and so palpably successful that they inevitably presented a challenge to the older notions of intellectual and public performance. The day had passed, wrote Émile Durkheim, for the man intellectually detached from all and interested in all; the individual capable of appropriating and expressing all that was "best" in civilization no longer had a place.[1]

In a larger sense the effect of these changes was to unsettle the aristocratic models of "civilized" existence which had for so long dominated European society (and which in unexpected ways it would now be the intellectual's lot to protect). It also raised the altogether new question, peculiar perhaps to a self-consciously and "philosophically" industrious age, of the productivity of the mind itself and of the possibility of looking upon the intellect as a productive unit with a measurable output. The scandal and alarm among men of letters at this suggestion are expressed by Isaac Disraeli, father of the celebrated statesman, in the following way:

A new race of jargonists, the barbarous metaphysicians of political economy, have struck at the essential existence of the production of genius in literature and art. . . . Absorbed in the contemplation of material objects, and rejecting whatever does not enter into their own restricted notion of "utility" these cold arithmetical seers, with nothing but millions in their imagination, and whose choicest works of art are spinning-jennies, have valued the intellectual tasks of the library and the studio by "the law of supply and demand." [2]

When Premier Guizot debated in parliament the electoral privileges of the intelligentsia he provided the social historian with a peculiarly French scene: an intellectual question argued at the highest levels of drama, rhetoric, doctrine, and politics. But we can recognize in Guizot's speech and in the issues to which it was addressed an episode in the general (and not yet ended) struggle over the peculiar demands and uncertain privileges of the modern intellectual. Disraeli's argument against the new barbarians had rested its case on the old-fashioned values of literary charm and uplift. Actually, however, the ultimate point at stake was whether or not the new literary elite which had emerged out of the social changes of the eighteenth and nineteenth centuries was to have a legitimate public place and whether people would bow before the accomplishments of this new and self-appointed aristocracy as they had once before bowed before their traditional or hereditary social betters.

In dealing with the tactics and issues of this question so dominant in their lives, the fear and anger of even the most diverse writers seemed always to lead to the same target—the middle class. This was true of Marx and Baudelaire, of romantics and revolutionists. Alexis de Tocqueville, a conservative and finely-bridled mind, and Louis Blanc, a partisan and libertarian one, could without strain agree on the moral shortcomings of the bourgeoisie in something like the same language. And if two men as far apart in their intellectual and social inclinations as de Tocqueville and Blanc could find themselves in the same company when confronted with this common object of denunciation, again the question arises of how a class which had so successfully climbed to political and economic power could also be regarded as the culturally underprivileged segment of society, to be placed beyond all historical dignity or spiritual virtue.

The tradition of spiritual suspicion of the middle class is, as we have seen, much older than the attacks of the intellectuals of the nineteenth century. Huizinga and Groethuysen found in royal annals and church records a portrayal of the French middle class as the vehicle of the lesser values of mankind. One medieval poet, Thomasin von Zilcaria, described the rise of the bourgeoisie in his time by saying that stools had climbed on tables, silver fir had descended to the valleys, and moss had ascended to the mountains. Another, Freidank, excluded the bourgeoisie from the God-intended social order which, as the poet understood it, was constituted by the peasantry, the knighthood and the priesthood.[3] In England, as in France, it had been possible for men starting in the market place to acquire a reasonably good name or, as one seventeenth-century writer put it, "by good husbandry, and thriftie course of Trading, to raise themselves from meane estates . . . to be potent and mightie."[4] Nevertheless, in order to attain final acceptance, successful business and professional men in both these countries often reached for the cultural and material appurtenances of the aristocracy, including the belated acquisition of "ancestral" lands. In Cobbett's time stock jobbers, merchants, and professional people could not wait to acquire deer parks, mansions, and artificial ruins for their gardens, and insurance men had their portraits painted in hopeful imitations of the pointed sobriety of barons and squires. As late as the 1860's Anthony Trollope wrote that "the name of the land is still great in England," a reflection of the fact that, as the sociologists Lewis and Maude put it, the banker turned nobleman was always the nobleman turned land-owner.[5] In Voltaire's France, as we have seen, neither money nor business eminence alone was enough to gain social esteem, not even from the point of view of the rich themselves.

In the hands of nineteenth-century writers this tradition of intellectual contempt for the bourgeoisie became not only an attitude of dismissal, but a habit of implacable accusation. The anti-bourgeois credo took many forms—rage, an air of long-suffering endurance before bourgeois crassness, a tone of savage patronizing—but all of them were at the bottom predicated on the same aristocratic principle of social ranking. This principle received many elaborations, aesthetic and psychological, but its ideological import can perhaps be best understood by recalling the public sentiments which in the past have served as the actual foundation of aristocracy as a social system. And to do this, nothing is more expedient than to turn to Thorstein Veblen's *The Theory of the Leisure Class,* not so much as an essay on the sociological drama of money and prestige, nor as a topical satire on the American tycoon (although it is both of these) but as a treatise on the concept of aristocratic behavior and its relation to work, productivity, and spiritual excellence.

Though lack of historical and sociological precision is the great shortcoming of Veblen's book, suggestiveness is its great virtue. Both these features combine to offer a description of certain broad historical trends which are relevant to us here. Under the earliest conditions, what Veblen calls "savagery," mankind was socially, economically, and psychologically collectivistic. It had no strong concept of individual ownership; it was peaceful, sedentary, lacked a dominant elite, and recognized no distinctions of dignity or indignity among occupations or kinds of work. This primitive way of life was replaced by "barbarism," a social order resulting from the practice of social aggression, that is, war and conquest, and whose economic system rests on the labor of war captives. Men, the perpetrators of these depredations, were the first masters; women were often the first captives to have their labor exploited regularly for the benefit of their captors. Women, therefore, became one of the earliest forms of personal property. Hence "barbaric" society regarded virtually all provisions of goods and services as a symbolic extension of female work, and this in turn laid the foundation of a long-lasting social habit which views all servitude and all routine forms of work as peculiar to captive souls who are tamed, housebroken, and in some sense emasculated. In its lower stage "barbarism" did not possess a fully developed leisure class, although it began some of the moral and cultural distances which were later to separate worthy from unworthy behavior (for example, hunting, a practical and customary means of gathering food at this time, was regarded not as industrious drudgery but as a form of prowess). In the final or "high" stage of barbarism, however, a definite aristocracy developed whose tastes and privileges were specifically nonindustrious— war, rulership, sports, and the priesthood. These were formally nonindustrious but also, because of their roots in male predatory powers (men, says Veblen, are always the inchoate aristocracy), they were not only honorable but specifically masculine.[6]

These are, of course, sweeping though catchy speculations. They are not, on the other hand, flagrant inventions, and something like what they describe can be recognized in the history of Western culture, both pre-Christian and Christian. But because they are intended to embrace the whole history of social relations (jumping from Oriental to European societies without much hesitation) and cannot be tied to specific proof, Veblen has sometimes been accused of bogus and opportunistic scholarship. Such a view humorlessly misses the point. Veblen's accounts are really theoretical evocations aimed above all at uncovering the symbolic content of our social heritage. Who could deny, for example, that the taboo-like indignity of some jobs and occupations in present-day society stem from the generic quality of womanly domesticity attached to them? Or (and this is one of Veblen's most inspired generalities) that our "uncreative" work such as is reserved for laboring classes represents not only a form of social but of spiritual inferiority, and that we look upon such inferiority as the product of an inner inanimateness and brutishness just as we look upon nonutilitarian occupations (like war and religion) as natural instances of spiritual exertion and moral deed?

All of Veblen's famous book is in one sense an effort to answer a remarkable question not regarded before him as sociologically significant. Why was it that the daily acts of human productiveness, the very tasks essential to the survival of society, were precisely those which society refused to regard as honorific? In tracing the sources of this paradox Veblen scattered through the early portion of *The Theory of the Leisure Class* a number of thoughts which may be brought together into the following chart of related categories of the honorable and the dishonorable.

Honorable	*Dishonorable*
Man-work	Woman-work
Nonproductive work (exploit)	Productive work (drudgery)
Spiritual activity	Spiritual inertness
Freedom	Servitude
Uniqueness	Routine
Individuality	Collectivity
	Impersonality

In other words the honorable categories are the "masculine" ones: contempt for normalcy, unique emotions, strong passions, and special deeds. This was, as we remember, just the scale of values against which at least one aspect of nineteenth-century literature sought to measure the bourgeoisie's lack of human nobility. Indeed it does not take too much to see that one major phase of romanticism, the romanticism of Byron and Hugo among others, is inseparable from the figure of the magically powerful male adventurer, a figure so durable that one may say that in a variety of banal manifestations, including banal brutality, the romantic hero is still the hero of popular literature.

Yet this view of the traditions of the creative life as a symbolic restatement of acts of exploit in the Veblenian sense of the latter term raises certain obvious historical questions. Before the romantic age, women served as the carriers of culture, the experts in sensitivity, and the organizers of the participation of the family in civilized life. When one looks, for instance, at the salons of the French eighteenth century, one finds their administration typically divided between the husband, as the investor who unwillingly foots the bill, and the wife as the master of ceremonies who stage-manages the gathering of literary, scientific, and artistic lights. Indeed, some anecdotes of the period treat the relationship between intellectuals and fashionable women as that of natural partners in the game of imagination and taste, while husbands appear as both skillful moneymen and sleepy-minded bores lost amidst the wit and elegance of their wives' guests.* The husbands are in this respect very much like the vegetative businessmen of nineteenth-century satire. The parlor intellectuals, on the other hand, seem much too bright and polished to reflect the Veblenian concept of male prowess. If anything they appear closer to their patrons in the effeminacy suggested by their concern with graciousness and charm, personal as well as literary.

Veblen himself offers the way out of the difficulty presented by the historical existence of "feminine" forms of aristocratic life. For there are in Veblen two theories of the formation and the characteristics of cultural elites. The first one, already discussed, is created by the practitioners of individual prowess, spiritual and physical. The second corresponds to periods of economic plenty during which, after protracted contact with accumulated wealth and unbroken privilege, the socioeconomic elite would develop a cultural manner dedicated to the aesthetic elaboration of leisure, creating a world, Veblen said, capable of tolerating breaches of faith but never breaches of decorum.[7] Veblen seemed to attach no particular chronology to the emergence of styles of life dominated by the spirit of courtly form. Highly complex social manners and the cultivation of non-utilitarian skills and tastes (including such things as art collect-

---

* In Marguerite Glotz and Madeleine Marie's *Salons du XVIIIe siècle* this story is told. Mme. Geoffrin, the leader of a celebrated salon, was married to a wealthy businessman who attempted to resist his wife's expenditures on cultural affairs. However, Mme. Geoffrin, "with her Alexander-like soul," won and turned her house into one of the great intellectual establishments of Paris. One day, after a long absence of Monsieur Geoffrin, it occurred to one of his wife's regular guests to ask, "What became of that old gentleman who always sat at the head of the table without saying anything?" "That was my husband," Mme. Geoffrin answered. "He is dead."

ing and the value of a "classical education") were part of the
leisure class rituals of "conspicuous consumption." In Veblen's
sense, we could find such pursuits and tokens of class well-
being and refinement equally among the European nobility of
the past, the plantation aristocracy of the American South, and
the business elite of the American North during the latter's
great period of social splendor and cultural expenditure in the
early part of this century. In its purely intellectual and artistic
aspects, however, Veblen's concept of the polite society would
seem to have its most complete expressions in the Renaissance
and Classical periods of European cultural history, particularly
French classicism, in which the spirit of courtiership and the
concern for the formal perfecting of human experience, both
inward and outward, were the object of unparalleled literary
and aesthetic dedication.

If the Renaissance and the Classical Age embodied the intellectual content of one aristocratic model, romanticism may be
said to stand as the ideological symbol of another and earlier
form of aristocracy corresponding to what Veblen calls "high
barbarism." Veblen describes the high-barbarian aristocratic
type as the protagonist of two forms of prowess: the inner personal possession of transcendental mysteries—religious superiority—and individual assertion over the run of mankind by
virtue acts of physical domination or the thrust of an over-
powering will. Like "high barbarism," Romanticism glorified
introspection or impulse; and romantic freedom, like "high
barbarian" freedom was above all the freedom to act in a
singular, even in an instinctual way. Romantic intellectual pride
is the pride that attaches to wholly individualized dexterity or
to purely personal spiritual possessions, and which, consequently,
must deny worth to all those who are bound to routine duties.
Freedom, therefore, in this subjective sense of the "barbaric," is
an essentially expressive thing which transcends the psychological and, because it is always a nonproductive discharge of
energy, even the biological demands of daily life. Freedom is

glorious because it is "creative," and it is "creative" because it constitutes a display of gratuitous personal originality. By contrast, labor is repressive and inglorious because it is spiritually unfree and condemns its servants to a compulsive monotony. Freedom, which is the realm of spontaneity, generates and presumes peculiarity; work is the lot of the undifferentiated masses.

From these psychological and aesthetic points of view, therefore, the romantic-barbarian conception of aristocracy entails a distinction between creativity and productivity that has remained prominent until today. Romanticism set the terms of contemporary traditions of creativity in that it celebrated either the heroic or the intimate, the impulses that put man that side of workaday reality by entirely overriding it, or this side of it by withdrawal into a purely personal world. Creativity in this sense relates only to actions which are individual and, in a literal sense, incomparable. As a statement of art, as a manifestation of sensitivity or as actual behavior, creativity is in this tradition always self-bound and always self-determined. It cannot be experienced, expressed or produced in similar or equal parts by a collectivity. It cannot be measured in terms of something other than itself. It is of a piece. It has integrity. To understand this is also to understand why literary artists, who could never find a good word for the middle class, were always able to praise themselves or traditional societies, that is, the individual capable of creating or expressing an intellectual or aesthetic whole or a traditional collectivity (whether this was represented by tribal life, village folk, or an aristocratic class) faithful to a fully developed and stable inheritance. The creative individual and the traditional community were the possessors of different forms of cultural completeness, the protagonists of finished cultural styles containing within themselves a depth of particular values.* Considering the force of this belief, one should not be

* Daniel Lerner in his recent *The Passing of the Traditional Society* (Glencoe, Illinois: The Free Press, 1958) makes a similar distinction be-

surprised to discover that literary men in the nineteenth century were often more profoundly repelled by the psychological and cultural features of the bourgeoisie, the inherent valuelessness of their lives and the internal anonymity of their souls, than by their moral sins such as their presumed exploitative instincts. W. H. Auden, explaining why the poetic temper is drawn to people like great warriors, athletes, heiresses, descendants of well-bred families, or even monomaniacs and big-time gangsters, says that for the poet mankind is divided into two sorts: the gifted few whom he admires because they are "really themselves" (Auden might have said with Shakespeare that they are "the lords and owners of their faces"), and the average mass who are "no one in particular." [8] Contemplating this "unbeing" of the noncreative person Flaubert could only throw up his arms, amazed and uncomprehending. What did people not concerned with art do? E. E. Cummings, asking himself what happens to those who are not artists, concluded simply that "nothing" happens to them.[9]

The industrious man who shouldered his way into the leadership of modern society threatened all three ideals of intellectual aristocracy—the heroic, the formal, and the introspective. But the threat was not only to the spiritual hierarchies. By making new and unexpected demands on human vitality modern pragmatism was also likely to undermine man's total sensitivity, his emotional free play, and that capacity for physical pleasure which in the past had represented a means both of biological and of aesthetic fulfillment. When Stendhal, as he traveled through a Europe emerging into the industrial age, remarked that one of the consequences of the modern dedication to

tween at least one version of the traditional society and the rationalistic-materialistic (that is, bourgeois) character of modern society. Traditional society is symbolized by what he calls The Chief, a cultural style based on reverence for ancestry, custom, and such nonutilitarian virtues as honor and courage. Modern culture is the culture of what Lerner calls The Grocer, the "ingenuity culture" of men thirsty for change and social advance through the acquisition and manipulation of commodities.

productivity was sure to be the exhaustion of the natural human gift for the enjoyment of life, he did not mean, as we do today, that men should aim at a busy existence soundly balanced by needed and calculated distraction. He was speaking rather of the decline in the free aesthetics of human amiability which traditionally and unselfconsciously men had blended with their necessary tasks, of the erosion of man's capacity for sensuous and erotic escape from routine, of the obliteration of the psychological open spaces of daily life.

In making such observations Stendhal was voicing the intuition, common to literary men and social analysts, that modern life imposes upon men a choice between original and intense experience (psychological and biological) and the demands of social utility. Veblen suggests something like this as an element in the processes of class differentiation when he contrasts the thrust and potency of primitive aristocracies with the regimented acquiescence to productive tasks of those whose duty it is to provide society with the means of material subsistence (it should be clear, of course, that Veblen was himself against waste and in favor of productivity; he had nothing to say about pleasure). For Stendhal, however, the novelty of modern economic and occupational conditions was that they extended hard work to all social classes, including the higher ones. Freud, it seems, also assumed this to be the case when he discussed the conflict between the claims of pleasure and the requirements of social effectiveness. This opposition had two principal manifestations: one was the diversion of psychological impulses away from personal gratification and toward beneficent but abstract social relations such as humanitarianism*; the other was the necessity to choose between industriousness

* Freud did not say, like George Orwell, that every humanitarian was a hypocrite. He felt, however, that broad and righteous social concerns were substitutes for a personal sense of erotic inadequacy; in "loving" humanity we were always assured that our love would be returned because the object of that love was no one in particular, but an indeterminate "All."

and eroticism demanded by the fact that men possessing limited libidinal powers must apportion these powers among their various tasks, so that, as society became a more complex and engaged more of men's efforts in social enterprise, it required a corresponding withdrawal of energy from sexual functions.[10] As the money bags in Balzac's novel *Gobseck* understood it, the choice was between "powerful emotions which use up one's strength or . . . regular occupations which make life an English machine that does its work in a given time." [11]

Although Freud saw the standardization of sexual practice into monogamy as a problem for modern society (since there was no comparable uniformity of sexual temperament in all men)—he said that the constraints of civilization might actually disable people sexually—he did not separate the sexual impulse from the interests of the family. However, for men with utopian, artistic or, in Freud's terms, "narcissistic" views of sexuality, the conflict was bound to appear extreme. Baudelaire, for instance, thought that no one could be a businessman and a lover because devotion to love-making, not as a domestic obligation but as an artistic expression of the sensuous self, required first of all freedom from the necessity of earning a living. This dream of an elegant sexual holiday is, of course, typically "Baudelairian," but the suggestion of a subterranean liaison between sensuality and spirituality, which has been a part of Western literary imagination since the Romantic movement, links the psychological intuitions of Romanticism with the essence of Freudian psychology. This link makes it possible for us now to read back from psychoanalysis into the nineteenth century, and to understand why writers of that period came to form an image of the businessman in which material success was inseparable from spiritual and biological shortcomings—a sedentary, unerotic, and anti-vital type, carpet slippers and all.

Since symbols will nurture their own countersymbols it is understandable that the aesthetic imagination of the nineteenth

century should have sought a foil against which to set its model
for the literary hero. It found it in the philosopher of thrift and
remunerative temperance, Benjamin Franklin. Stendhal saw in
the "Philadelphia artisan" the incarnation of utilitarian morality: the pious and successful bore.[12] Baudelaire made Franklin part of a little and unfinished sketch on the downfall of
the aristocratic spirit entitled *The Last of Don Juan.* The characters—there are only two, Don Juan and his domestic Leporello—are barely outlined, but the thesis is unmistakable. Leporello is not only a servant. He is also, Baudelaire tells us,
imbued with the characteristic middle class passion to better his
condition by means of commerce. In this, he reminds us of
the Veblenian theme of the meniality of productivity. However, unlike Veblen's domestic, whose chief psychological
duty is to minister to the spiritual superiority of his master,
Leporello is a self-confident, hale, and vulgar upstart clearly
about to crowd his social superior off the historical stage. As
for the aristocrat, Baudelaire makes him not only a storied gentleman but a world-weary soul, thus suggesting to the reader
the incompatibility between the aristocratic spirit and the materialistic efficacy and optimism of the businessman. There was
also a point of sociopsychological history intended in the name
he chose for his gentleman: Don Juan, a name synonymous
with erotic glory. We are to understand, therefore, that the de-
feat of the gentleman at the hands of Leporello marks not only
the destruction of the aristocracy by the bourgeoisie but the
fall of Eros before the powers of the market place. At the end of
this little farce the mask comes off Leporello and his person
and significance are revealed to us as follows:

Cold, reasonable, and vulgar, he speaks of nothing but virtue and
economy, two ideas which he naturally associates. His mind is that
of Franklin. He is a knave in Franklin's style. He is the rising bourgeoisie come to replace the faltering aristocracy.[13]

One writer of our own times who also crowned Franklin as

the prince of the philistines is, not unexpectedly, D. H. Lawrence. Lawrence not only charged Franklin, as others before had, with a merchant's theology whose God was a "heavenly storekeeper."* He made a great deal of Franklin's presumed sexual pettifogging, inseparable in Lawrence's mind from Franklin's economic frugality; he viewed Franklin's recommendation to *use* (Lawrence's emphasis) sexuality for health and procreation as a singularly uproarious and disgusting joke.[14] †
Lawrence's most celebrated novel, *Lady Chatterley's Lover,* is an essay on the same essential theme: the attrition of primal experience under the tyranny of too narrow and deliberate a life purpose. The book's concern with sexuality is, as such, important, but it must be understood as part of Lawrence's mystical naturalism, which maintained that only by releasing man from the "will" and the "head" could a subtle and potent harmony be restored between him and the rest of the biological world. Lawrence, it should be pointed out, advocated sexual freedom in a psychological, not in a social sense. He was passionately partial to monogamy and thought Bernard Shaw a vicious vulgarian and pathological puritan for saying that prostitutes rather than priests should have the right to speak on matters of sex. The Pope in Rome, Lawrence said, knew more about sex than the emancipated Shaw, for the Pope regarded physical union as a sacrament while Shaw, the atheist, saw it only as purchasable stimulation. Indeed, Lawrence upheld the right of the clergy to prohibit bare arms in church because this showed that, even considered as obscenity or blasphemy, erot-

* This peculiar equation of piety and profit, which appeared to literary men as the key to the business personality, would of course become a famous scholarly thesis with Max Weber, who himself found in Benjamin Franklin the archetype of modern economic ethics. Max Weber, *The Protestant Ethic and the Spirit of Capitalism* (New York: Scribner's Sons, 1930).

† What the historical Franklin really was like is not pertinent to the meaning of the symbol. In Weber's terminology, Stendhal, Baudelaire, and Lawrence saw Franklin as the "ideal type" bourgeois, though they built this type on literary intuition rather than historical evidence.

icism was a religious question. He himself saw such displays as marks of frivolous lust and, therefore, as cynical and "atheistic." [15]

Lady Chatterley proposes the overcoming of prudery in marriage so that lust and frivolity may be cured and instinct ("blood") restored to a sound role in human relations. This restoration, however, requires a denial of the entire inheritance of rationalism and particularly a rejection of industrialization. Lawrence's position before rationalism as a philosophical principle was the position held by European romanticism since the beginning of the nineteenth century. Rationalism was a pretentious and naïve dogma which subjected the deeper forms of human understanding to the tyranny of naked calculation. Business and industrialization were the social children of such a spirit. More than that, they were the claws with which rationalism put nature and feeling under the abasing power of the machine and the abstract commands of the market. This imposition of the calculating will on man his living surroundings was, in Lawrence's mind, the most self-destructive of all of man's "triumphs." It separated him from the partnership of nature and, in so doing, produced a peculiar sense of privation and loneliness not to be appeased by the mechanistic greed for still further domination of which modern man had become the self-driven slave.

Considering the economic problems of a rising population and the indigence ruling many parts of the world, Lawrence's ideas may appear as rampant foolishness and obscurantism: romanticism in the most obnoxious and childish sense of the term. Yet we may put it in a more understandable light by setting aside Lawrence's description of machinery as the perpetrator of a carnage upon nature, and thinking of what he has to say about the psychology of modern productivity, his fear that machinery suppressed a total relationship to the surroundings which would embrace the biological and aesthetic as well as the productive, and his fear that this suppression sapped man's sense of organic integrity, thus committing him to an arid and single-minded pursuit of external manipulation. As he put it in *Lady Chatterley*, it took the destruction of the living, intuitive faculty to release the uncanny will power needed for industrial organization.[16]

A spiritual danger in the process of rationalized economics other than the disruption of the aesthetical-biological relationship between man and nature was the dislocation of the natural bond among men. This is an issue not unknown to sociolgists, among whom it takes the form of a concern with the dissolution of cultural intimacy and homogeneity under the conditions of urban industrial society. In *Lady Chatterley*, too, the theme of social rationalization parallels the theme of the destruction of personal communication and especially of what Lawrence regards as the latter's most mystically complete expression, sexual communication. As Lawrence's novel takes us through the mining town of Tevershall, we see everything, dwellings as well as landscape, lying under the lifeless detritus of industrial ravenousness. Walls, roofs, pavement, even mud are penetrated by coal dust. Everything displays "the utter negation of natural beauty, the utter negation of the gladness of life, the utter absence of the instinct of shapely beauty, which every beast and bird has." [17] And as we come to know the mine owner, Sir Clifford, we discover a man deprived of the bounty of human intimacy and literally a sexual cripple. The fact that this disablement is the product of a war wound might make us doubt the psychological intention of Sir Clifford's handicap. Lawrence himself seems at first to have been doubtful about its meaning. However, as he thought of Clifford, he came to see his wound as symbolic of a certain modern condition. He wrote in *A Propos Lady Chatterley's Lover:*

. . . [T]he novel was written from start to finish three times. And when I read the first version, I recognized that the lameness of Clifford was symbolic of the paralysis, of the deeper and passional paralysis of most men of his sort today.[18]

In portraying the threat posed to man by modern techniques, particularly the threat to the erotic foundations of his life, Lawrence perhaps unintentionally tends to suggest an opposition between productivity and humanity. It is not difficult to see why this should be so because, from such points of view as we have been considering, most attempts to discuss "meaningful" sorts of productivity must almost inevitably lead to nostalgic forms of economic imagination. One example of this is found in the writings of Arthur Miller. Miller has been surrounded with a certain revolutionary aura in the conventional political sense. Actually, however, he speaks for the ideals of an earlier social order. His values are the values of craftsmanship and the principle of a sustained personal relationship to the act of production which presumably existed in a craft society. As a practical possibility such an ideal may be a lost cause. It is, nevertheless, capable of exerting a powerful dramatic appeal which serves to uncover yet other troubled thoughts about the cultural and spiritual dangers of modern production. If we were to outline the economic morality implicit in Miller's *Death of a Salesman,* it would appear to be something like this. Men can develop relationships of integrity with other men by exchanging moral values and psychological and social benefits, such as companionship, affection, and solidarity. Men also can have relationships of integrity to objects, provided these objects represent an act of human expression as well as production; that is to say, that they stand for creativity as well as productivity. When the product represents an outcome of the maker's skills and values, it constitutes also a statement of the maker's person. The buyer who acquires such a product becomes an "audience," the recipient of a creative service and, therefore, as the selector of the object, himself the performer of a creative act. Thus a marketing exchange may be turned into an exchange of human and aesthetic values. What characterizes modern manufacturing, however, is the spiritually empty relationship of the producer to the product. This is equally and perhaps more profoundly true of the subject of Miller's play, the salesman. Nothing in the personal reality of the salesman attaches itself to the product because he is neither creatively nor morally responsible for it. Therefore the salesman must shift from a significant relation to the product to a pseudo-significant relation to the customer (only a really significant relation to the product could, of course, be the basis of a genuine relation to the customer). The act of selling must in consequence turn on a deliberate pretense of human motives—that ingenious and degraded travesty of human relations known as "selling oneself." * It is Miller's point that the ultimate victim of this fraud is the salesman himself and that the outcome of a life of hollow and strenuous pseudo-sociability employed as a lubricant for marketing can only be despair and, finally, self-destruction.[19]

Although Miller is clearly in the tradition of those who hold commerce incapable of creating a dignified human purpose, he is not so much concerned with the stigma of utility as with the market's tragic futility. His salesman, Willy Loman, is haunted by the ghost of his brother and puzzled and defeated by the bitter hostility of his son. The brother went as a young man to seek his fortune on the Alaskan frontier, a stage for real trials and real victories ("That was a Man!" Willy says of him). Biff, the son, refuses his father's advice to put youth and good looks at the service of salesmanship. The frontiersman brother embodies the standard American version of the heroic; the son speaks not only for the revulsion against personality marketing but against white-collar and factory discipline and for the re-

* It should be clear that in all of this one must see a scheme of intellectual responses to the intellectual's own image of the market, not a historically realistic description of the market itself. Craftsmanship and its time have been idealized in literature since the nineteenth century. However, as C. G. Coulton and other historians have shown, the very high standards of craft imposed by medieval guilds often had to do with such purely economic considerations as control over the membership or of prices and the elimination of competitors. This does not discount, of course, the pride of the craftsman in his traditional skill.

turn to an earlier, more "creative" economic ideal—he wants to live outdoors, whistle on the job, and do something he "likes to do." The son and the brother are "real" (even though the latter is a ghost). Willy is "unreal" and in the end succumbs to his own unreality. Much like the suicides of Émile Durkheim's studies, he kills himself because he has lost the capacity for concrete psychological and social possessions.[20]

Death of a Salesman, accomplishes the reduction of the conflict between "being" and "doing" to its most graspable terms. The play's lesson is that there cannot be a constructive and permanent human attachment to the market; the market is ephemeral and it renders man ephemeral. Willy, who has successfully thrown himself into the bargain a thousand times, disintegrates the moment he cannot sell his merchandise. In many ways his life has no real history. There is in him no rise of individuality, no self-investment and, consequently, no self-possession. In the end, when he is discarded because his personality credit is exhausted, he must destroy himself.

Another manifestation of the flight from the spiritual atmosphere of modern productivity is the emergence of what may be called intellectual tribalism. This is a development with at least two principal manifestations. One is the self-consciously archaic return to primitivism (sometimes symbolically, sometimes actually), to a world where no men or values are for sale, to a society where life has undefiled honesty and spontaneous beauty. Another manifestation, distinguished from the first in that it is not necessarily anachronistic or, in an obvious sense, primitive, is the search for the company of men possessed of an inborn Bohemianism and an incapacity for the understanding of business values. Historically, intellectual tribalism has taken a number of guises. Flaubert, for example, sometimes painted primitive societies as being as world-weary as himself (he imagined that nomads wandered out of melancholy rather than economic necessity), sometimes bathed them in the enameled *Orientalisme* fashionable in his day. D. H. Lawrence, on the other hand, was more thoughtful and serious and produced, in one instance, accounts of Pueblo ceremonies which the anthropologist Ruth Benedict greeted as peculiarly faithful to the spirit of that culture.[21]

The first dreams of literary tribalism were of the East and the American Indian. Later came the long history of celebration of the gypsies, both in popular romance in high literature. Flaubert admired gypsies as people whose mere survival constituted a threat and an affront to the ideals of bourgeois society. Later eccentric scholars, artists, and poets, from George Borrows in the nineteenth century to Augustus John and García Lorca in our day, praised them as spiritual friends and companions and made them the subjects of some of their best work. Curiously, the literature of the United States, the great middle-class nation, is uniquely rich in such legendary anti-bourgeois communities, both urban and rural. There are the affectionate, joyful, comfortably irresponsible *paisanos* of Steinbeck's *Tortilla Flat*. There are the California Armenians of William Saroyan, a sturdy yet whimsical peasantry. There is the colorful and tragic Negro microcosmos of Du Bose Heyward's *Catfish Row* (the source of Gershwin's *Porgy and Bess*). There is the cozily unorthodox household of Martin Vanderhoff, in Hart and Kaufman's *You Can't Take It with You,* in whose living room "meals are eaten, plays are written, snakes collected, ballet steps practiced, xylophones played, printing presses operated." [22] In every case, the dream is the same. The disreputable, the useless, and the outcast become the core of a citizenry of human "truth," freed of the materialistic pretense as well as the shallow anxieties of the middle-class world.

Now, because every generation must experience its own rebellion as a new thing, it is understandable that some contemporary writers would think of their anger and aloneness as belonging only to themselves. For instance, in *The White Negro,* a well-known essay on the American Bohemia following World War II, the novelist Norman Mailer explains the main protagonist of that Bohemia, the native "existentialist" and itinerant nihilist known as the hipster, as the product of social brutalization in a totalitarian era, the threat of human extinction by new instruments of war, and the uncontrollable expansion (irrespective of political ideologies) of the powers of the state over the individual. Mailer thinks also that this Bohemia finds its hero in the Negro, seeks the Negro's sexual freedom, imitates his speech, and worships his music (jazz) because, having lived for two hundred years in a subworld "between democracy and totalitarianism," the Negro has become a natural social adventurer sworn against respectability, comformity, dullness, and emotional timidity.[23]

As a description of the language and the experience of today's literary derelicts in the United States, *The White Negro* is skilled and eloquent. But Mailer's historical explanations are either too modest or simply misplaced. When one first reads a "hipster" writer like Jack Kerouac he sounds indeed like one of Mailer's spiritual nonwhites wanting to exchange places with the happy "true-hearted" Negroes of America. But there is more.

At lilac evening I walked with every muscle aching among the lights of 27 and Welton in the Denver colored section, wishing I were a Negro, feeling that the best the white world had offered was not enough ecstasy for me, not enough life, joy, kicks, darkness, music, not enough night. I stopped at a little shack where a man sold red-hot chili in paper containers; I bought some and ate it, strolling in the dark, mysterious streets. I wished I were a Denver Mexican, or even a poor overworked Jap, anything but what I was so drearily, a "white man disillusioned." [24]

It is well-intended but implausible for Mailer to attribute this spiritual exodus across racial lines to such things as atomic fission and totalitarianism. Equally unlikely is Mailer's explanation of the Negro's presumed gift of lustiness and unconventionality as a product of a "totalitarian" spirit. First of all, nothing is so evident in the passage just quoted from Kerouac's novel, *On the Road,* as the survival of the romantic tradition of the nineteenth century in the world of the hipster. In the true personalistic vein of romanticism, Kerouac's complaint is not about social justice but about spiritual nakedness; he would rather be exploited than bored. Ecstasy is inescapably there, as is darkness, both as a hunger for mystery and as a refuge from the glaring and prodding "purposefulness" of rationalized society.

Actually, as the liquidation of the Hungarian gypsies by the Nazis clearly shows, totalitarian societies are intolerant of unorganizable folk traditions and "wasteful" cultural peculiarities, both of which the Negro has richly developed in the course of his American experience; the liquidation of the Hungarian gypsies by the Nazis certainly shows that. Besides, the existence of massive racial tensions in the United States, as everyone must realize, is due to discrimination as well as to the invitation daily extended to Negroes, by public ideology, political institutions, and a constantly changing social climate, to assert their claims on American life. Finally, it is clear that the white-Negro ideal is not a Negro but a white-outsider ideal.* If there is a revolution among American Negroes today it is the revolution of respectability—not the struggle for a greater erotic freedom or a more imaginative way of life, but a struggle for the privileged anxieties of economic and professional success.

Despite Mailer's inadequacies as a social theorist, his profile of the hipster expands the history of anti-business types, not only because of the characteristics of the hipster himself, but because of those of the hipster's enemy, foil, and antipode, the square. The square, as we find him in Mailer and in other accounts of the hipster world such as Lawrence Lipton's *The Holy Barbarians*,[25] is of course first of all a conformist; he has that particular capacity for embracing social conventions to be ex-

---

* Of Kerouac's conception of Negro life the Negro writer James Baldwin has written: "I would hate to be in Kerouac's shoes if he should ever be mad enough to read this aloud from the stage of Harlem's Apollo Theater." *Time,* May 17, 1963, p. 23.

pected in the "success-oriented" man. To the hipster, on the contrary, men who profess to uphold "social" standards or posture as servants of the community are either bores or self-appointed frauds. Therefore, while the square is always an astringent and righteous prig, or at best a crassly jovial huckster, the hipster is marked by a fundamentally ironic imagination, a subtle funny bone which keeps him from embracing obviously respectable values or any other form of social pretense.

Now, if one face of the hipster is detachment, the other is his gift for torrential and transcending experience (erotic or aesthetic), his head-on embracing of life, or his capacity for some telling form of musing or contemplation. And this, correspondingly, exposes another side of the square's personality, that is to say, his emotional cautiousness, his calculation and opportunism, his lack of biological intensity, and a wholly personal style of expressiveness, all of which are part of the price which the square must pay for social and economic adjustment. The hipster (or beat) Bohemian, like all Bohemians, aims at being the total personal embodiment of his own ideals. The entire rhythm and effect of his behavior must reflect the ease and freedom of his withdrawal from the commonplace, his surrender to genuine experience, or his taking deep possession of that experience. The square, on the contrary, is marked by his gracelessness and by that absence of a ready individual intensity inevitable in someone who uses his personality as a social investment rather than as an independent creative experiment.

There seems to be a fairly widespread and intuitive recognition in the United States of the fundamental social attitudes represented by the hipster and the square, and of the depth of the duality between them (a duality which may sometimes coexist within the same individual). At least it would seem so from the currency which these two terms have gained outside the hipster world itself. But the hipster-square duel serves also to clarify much that was obscure in the terminology of earlier literary discontent. Thus when we are told that the square is the man who is always in a rigid and unreleased bind, we know that we have encountered such a creature before. Flaubert, Stendhal, Hugo, Baudelaire, and their contemporaries made, as we know, large and voluble use of the word bourgeois. With it they spoke of a social class, a dimension of life, and a personality type. Flaubert, for instance, regarded as bourgeois all symbols of conformity and professional ambition ("as dully bourgeois as the wooden benches of the Law School"); the kind of imagination or lack of it that always insists on being "to the point" (he thought that some remarks of de Musset about inconsistencies in *Hamlet* were "utterly bourgeois"); the inability to understand certain forms of longing ("last night you jeered like a bourgeoise at the pathetic dreams I had when I was fifteen"), any desire for success, even intellectual success ("what makes me indignant is the bourgeoisisme of our fellow writers. Such businessmen. Such vulgar idiots. . . ."); the prestige-conscious culture fads of the ignorant and the insensitive ("if a critic says of a sculptor that 'he neglects form . . . but is a thinker,' " the bourgeois proceed "with cries of joy, to make themselves admire what really bored them"); the inability to rise above commonplace sentiment, personal or social (speaking of a visit to a lady friend whom he expected to find old and ugly he says: "a bourgeois would say that I'll be greatly disillusioned: But I have rarely experienced disillusion having had few illusions"); the inability to appraise aesthetically the quality of one's own behavior, even the most intimate (writing about his sister's burial to Maxime Du Camp he says: "I was dry-eyed as a tombstone, but horribly tense. I wanted to tell you this, thinking that it would give you pleasure. You are sufficiently intelligent, and love me enough to understand the word 'pleasure,' which would make a bourgeois laugh").[26] Such an array of meanings attached to one word makes it difficult to follow the enemies of the bourgeoisie through the history of their denunciations. As with the rebels of our own day, however, the answer with the nineteenth-century hunters of the bourgeois curse is that they knew what they meant; they knew that a word had been found to serve as tuning fork for a whole company of related images. The current cognate is humbler in origin than the historic epithet, but it is equally universal in intention. By comparing the two we know now that one thing that bourgeois meant was square.

In his recent collection of miscellaneous writings, *Advertisements for Myself,* Mailer makes a list of hip (the adjective for the noun hipster) concepts, notions, feelings, and images, and their square opposites, which makes the relationship between the historical and the present-day perceptions of the literary ideal and its enemies even clearer. Induction, says Mailer, is hip, and deduction is square. So with self as opposed to society, crooks to cops, saints to clergymen, body to mind, manners to morals, night to noon, questions to answers.[27] Since one of the things that Mailer intends is to celebrate the nonrational and to test our capacity for it, he rightly says nothing about the grounds for his choice. But these are not too difficult for us to guess at, partly because of the almost total intuitive felicity of Mailer's categories. We can perceive, for instance, that induction speaks for boldness of mind, for unfolding and many-sided possibilities, for gaining understanding through ambivalence, and touching with the aid of feeling on the pulse of the concrete and the living. There is in it the freedom, the excitement, and the taste of a personal appropriation of experience. Deduction, on the other hand, suggests a cramped, rigid, and naked intellectual style—"safe," reductionistic, and impersonal, dependent on accumulated fact. The crook is hip because he is a nay-sayer to market values and utilitarian regularity (he is a taker, not a producer, buyer, or seller), but beyond that because he is among those who believe in self-assertion at the risk of everything else, even self-destruction. Cops, on the other hand, are the officious servants of social conformity. Saints are hip, because they are men "infatuated with self-perfection," sacred eccentrics; at the same time clergymen are predictably pious tenants of what Max Weber calls routinized transcendence. The body is hip because it represents the breathing, total reality of life impulses with all their secrets and irresistibility. The mind is square because it represents what Freud calls the "procrastinating factor of thought," [28] that is, caution, calculation, and the element of distance and control which comes with abstraction. Manners are hip because they have to do with the aesthetic organization of the self's personality style. Morals are a response to community demands. Night is the hour of intellectual secrecy, intimation, and withdrawal, when the hidden is released and the prohibited beseeched, therefore hip. Noon is the hour of explicit activity, of visible participation in the fabric and rhythm of social life, the hour of the repression of the obscure, the hour of money, normality, and work, therefore square. A question is hip because it is in itself disquieting, unfinished and beckoning, and, when truly a pure question, does not go beyond the flow and counterflow of wondering. An answer kills suspended experience by reducing the question to measurable terms. It forecloses the state of wondering. It de-individualizes and socializes experience by solving the problem and, therefore, creating the possibility of pragmatic action.*

One could replace "hip" and "square" by "romantic" and "bourgeois" and the equation would be the same. In both cases, personal life is always measured by the forays of the unmoored ego into self-expression, or its withdrawals into self-perception. On the other hand, participation in socialized activity threatens always to dismantle the irreducible "I" and to turn it into undifferentiated energy at the service of impersonal social usefulness. In either case what is denounced is the man of measurable ends, the undertaker of services (civil, mana-

---

* In the spirit of hipsterism the comedian-satirist Mort Sahl says of social problems: "After all, if we couldn't laugh about these things, we might do something about them." Cited in Robert Price, "The Fury," *The New Yorker,* July 1960, p. 40.

gerial, or economic), the careful and reliable personality, the job-performer, the producer; the "anal" man, in Freud's disquieting terminology.[29] When d'Alembert, a scientist and social philosopher, disapproved of a class like the flippant aristocracy of the later years of the Old Regime, he spoke of men who were "useless nullities whose scandalous luxury is an insult to the public." But when Stendhal or Flaubert speak of the bourgeoisie their tone is one of deep personal revulsion. Two stories of recent and past figures also show the difference in antibourgeois sentiments as they exist in the political and artistic worlds. In recalling his early acquaintance with Lenin, Leon Trotsky says that during the walks which the two would take around the city of London, Lenin would point out to him certain "capitalist" landmarks saying, "that's *their* House of Parliament, that's *their* Foreign Office." A contemporary of the painter Delacroix tells us that, although the artist's manners were impeccable, "he could hardly be polite to the middle classes." [30] The first of these anecdotes is "dialectical" in intention. Lenin speaks from without the walls of present powers but as the representative of a rising political force, a man already on the other side of the Marxist world-historical watershed looking on bourgeois institutions as still standing but irrevocably undermined. Delacroix's story has that intensely personal quality— the recoil from the commonplace as the first line of defense in the battle for spiritual dignity and self-identity—which is characteristic of bourgeois feelings rising out of cultural and aesthetic considerations.

At this point we must ask again: what is it in the spiritual scene of modern society that may account for such intellectual touchiness, willfulness, and bitterness? What made Flaubert say of all middle-class occupations that they were "little employments," or, of a magistrate friend, that his was an "idiotic" job worthy only of a cuckold? What made Baudelaire speak of the useful man as contemptible, or of all professions as the "stables of mankind?" The answer will be found only if we consider not only the middle class but something much more general of which the middle class may be an historical expression. This is the process of rationalization whose power to embrace and dominate social experience and purpose the nineteenth-century literary critics were among the first to perceive. If, for example, we take Mailer's one-word aphorisms for what they really are, which is to say one more statement of the romantic rejection of rationalism,* we will see also that they are directed at rationalism in at least two meanings of this word: rationalism as a philosophical method—the reduction of all experience to analytical terms—and rationalism as a social process, a process which, as Weber described it, tended to force all of human experience into a system of interrelated elements functioning according to procedures which led toward consistently predictable results. Weber regarded rationalism in this latter sense as the basic drift of modern society and described modern institutions as typically dominated by a rationalistic bias. The emergence of the legal foundations of the modern state, as distinguished from ancestral or purely personal forms of public authority, was one example of this historical process. Bureaucracy (public, private, political, or technological) with its insistence on fixed administrative formulas, regular duties, and authority based on trained skills rather than personal obligation or favor, was another.[31] Thorstein Veblen, too, observed that rationalization was the main feature of modernity, but he saw its chief instrument not in institutions, public or managerial, but in technology and its capacity to

---

* On the basis of philosophical or literary history it is of course impossible to make absolute distinctions between romanticism and its opposite, classicism, between feeling and reason, and so forth. No man, whether average or exceptional, could be exclusively one or the other. What is discussed here are ideological preferences and the deliberate attempt to further, cultivate, or glorify some intellectual features or denigrate others.

weigh, measure, test, classify, and manipulate the natural environment—and which, as a consequence, would not only render man's material existence orderly and predictable, but would make his intellectual life more objective and destroy "anthropomorphic" habits of thought.[32] Speaking of the Middle Ages and of the admiration which "reactionary" intellectuals felt for it, Marx remarked in *The Communist Manifesto* that what characterized medieval life from the point of view of productivity were "brutal" displays of vigor followed by periods of "the most slothful indolence." [33] For the romantic the oscillation between prowess and lassitude was intrinsically human and dramatically admirable. For Marx's philosophical and social rationalism it could only mean a wasteful management of social productivity. One feels, therefore, that Marx employed such words as "brutal" and "indolence" both angrily and carefully, in order to indicate the failure of the Middle Ages to use human energy in a rational and consistent fashion such as Marx had admired in the bourgeoisie and wished to extend to the whole of the social order.

Flaubert, as we remember, had discovered the spreading of the rationalistic spirit in every dominant phenomenon of modern life—in the psychological and moral characteristics of the bourgeoisie, in the structure of modern business and politics, and in the demands of the machine. And he saw it in the physical rhythm of human experience as dictated by such things as the tedious and compelling efficiency of modern highways.* Yet, even a man like John Stuart Mill, heir to a phil-

---

* Flaubert, however, was not the first writer to speak of roads as an example of the modern passion for cutting through the complexities of social existence and laying society bare to direct and simplified communication. Recalling the policies of the Old Regime, de Tocqueville, in 1856 (*The Old Regime and the French Revolution* [New York: Doubleday Anchor Books, 1955], p. 189.) wrote:

> The Highways Department was as fascinated then as it seems to be today by the perfectly straight line, and studiously avoided making use of existing roads if they showed

osophical and family tradition of social concern and alien to the strenuous aestheticsm which pervaded French literary arguments, concluded that certain forms of rationalism had pushed the question of personal freedom beyond such traditional arguments as that of the conflict between individual self-determination and political authority. As Mill saw it in 1859, freedom was now faced with an altogether novel danger which pressed on the psychological, emotional, and, so to speak, aesthetic rights of the person and which challenged his private imagination and his sense of being himself and no other as a spiritual and as a social actor; there was, said Mill, something "pinched, hidebound and narrow" in the modern "theory of life." This complaint may have in part originated with the merciless drilling in the right principles of human felicity which Mill received at the hands of his father. But this would only be a partial explanation. Mill (with so many others!) blamed Calvinism for maintaining that whatever was not duty was sin. However, he also suggested that peculiar forms of self-censorship were prompted by the mixed ambitions and uncertainties of modern life. There was in modern society, according to Mill, a curious sense of exposure which made each individual ask himself, not what was in accord with his personal disposition, but what suited his position—not what he might do as an individual, but was was usually done by persons of his station or, worse yet, what was usually done by persons of superior station and circumstance.[34] With observers of his own time, like de Tocqueville, and with sociologists of our own, Mill found a paradoxical partnership of comformity and social mobility which he stated as follows.

In whatever people do conformity is the first thing thought of; they like in crowds; they exercise choice only among things commonly done; peculiarity of taste, eccentricity of conduct, are

---

the slightest deviation from ideal rectitude. Rather than make a detour, however slight, our road makers hacked their way through ancient estates, defacing and destroying valuable parklands.

shunned equally with crimes; until by dint of not following their own nature, they have no nature to follow.[35]

According to Mill, therefore, modern society suffered from a scarcity of personal tastes and impulses, not from an excess of them. And he added to this an up-to-date-sounding note on the psychology of the mass society by explaining that men did not make commonplace choices out of hypocritical calculation but out of a genuine inability to chose, that is to say, out of a loss of personal character and individual impulse; "I do not mean that they choose what is customary in preference to what suits their own inclination. It does not occur to them to have any inclination, except for what is customary."[36]

It would be, of course, wrong and foolish to say that intellectual life is always unhappy, withdrawn, or dedicated to the perfecting of private dreams. Modern political rationalism, for example, was the creation of two great and optimistic intellectual dogmas: the liberal faith in the individual as capable of sorting out universally worthy aims for the conduct of human life and the socialist faith in "scientific" politics as the instrument of human justice and rationality. Yet even a writer like Mill, who cannot be accused of being a stereotypically wounded romantic soul, feared the consequences of rationalistic dictation for the meaning of personal experience. Automatons might as well grow corn and build houses, Mill said, in a world where human life was not "rightly employed in perfecting and beautifying . . . man himself."[37] And he asked for something better, as a guide to modern existence, than the views of "that very common character, the worshipper of 'our enlightened age' . . . struck by the multiplication of physical comforts, the advance in the diffusion of knowledge, the facilities of mutual intercourse, the great works accomplished throughout the globe by the cooperation of multitudes"; to take counsel from such a mind would be to succumb to "passionless stupidity" and to the desolation of a life dedicated to "executing by fixed rules fixed tasks."[38]

This battle against formlessness in human motivations and for the preservation of particularism in human experience developed through a series of changing aesthetic and intellectual perspectives. Thackeray, for example, spoke of the "mean admiration of mean things," by which he may have signified the growing dominance of plain but practical values of the kind which, according to Defoe, had made the middle class as socially powerful as it was personally dull and modest.[39] Flaubert, as we remember, felt that only the most defiant self-cultivation could avail the intellectual against the *arriviste* classlessness (and mindlessness) flooding society in the wake of democracy. But there were other resolves and other hopes. Art was enshrined by the nineteenth century because it embodied the concept of craft as the particular possession of an intellectual elite; it created objects which were supremely concrete and self-contained, free of the values of the market and representative of specific acts of intellectual and imaginative meaning. Sensuality was applauded, nursed, and flaunted because it shared with art the spirit of freedom and a completeness of experience which money could not buy. Stendhal's observation to the effect that the recruitment of energy for ever-increasing productivity and an ever-more complex organization of social life would have to occur at the expense of the senses might be thought frivolous by those who remember the calculated hedonism of Stendhal himself. It is really, however, a response to the historical parallel between the rise of modern social discipline, the appearance of doctrines aimed at curbing direct physical gratification, and the beginnings of modern industrialization. In his *Age of Louis XIV,* Voltaire said that the drawing of young noblemen into the salons of the seventeenth century and away from the brawling and debauchery of tavern life had been a great step in the development of a fitting style of genteel behavior.[40] *The Economist,* surveying, in 1851, "The First Half of the Nineteenth Century Progress of the Nation and the Race," saw the benefits of sobriety in a different light; the great strides of the century, *The Economist* said, were the creation of a spirit which had brought about equally the expansion of world trade and manufacturing, the abolition of slavery, the introduction of lighting, freedom of discussion, and the temperance movement.[41]

But it was not only the rationalism of busyness and occupational demands that was to be suspected. Duties, Robespierre had said at the height of Jacobinism, should be preferred to good manners and good company, and he had added that the mission of modern politics was "the guidance of human passions toward objects useful to public prosperity." [42] It is only in the light of such ideological pressure on the world of private pleasures and experiences that one can understand the quasi-religious flowering of romantic love in the nineteenth century, not only in its sentimental but also in its sociological significance. For love conceived in the romantic fashion is not only a personal impulse and need. It is also a deliberately goal-less and self-contained act of withdrawal from everything public—the ultimate statement of personal possession and personal surrender. Max Weber clearly understood this when he said that "the erotic relation seems to offer the unsurpassable peak of the fulfillment of the request of love in the direct fusion of the souls of one another. This boundless giving of oneself is as radical as possible in its opposition to all functionality, rationality and generality." [43]

However, the most elaborately staged reaction against "functionality" in all its forms and, in particular, against the social morality of the market, is perhaps to be found in Baudelaire's creation, the Dandy. The Dandy was the virtuoso of nonutilitarianism. He was the perfect example of life as a personal art. And his fanatical mannerisms can be understood only as a last-ditch psychological stand against the triumph of middle-class concepts of occupational dignity. In one of the most telling moments of the French Revolution, *The Declaration of the Night of August 4, 1797,* the National Convention abolished all feudal privileges and stated that "no useful profession shall imply the loss of honor." [44] Even before that, however, in his celebrated handbook on the historical aspirations of the bourgeoisie—*What Is the Third Estate?*—the Abbé Sieyès had claimed for it the right to represent the whole nation because the bourgeoisie performed labors which were "directly useful or agreeable to the person." [45] Speaking of the United States as a paradigm of democracy (in the sense of an order where every class tends to converge socially and politically toward some boundary-less middle ground), de Tocqueville once remarked that there all "honest" callings were regarded as "honorable," adding that, since physical well-being appeared to such societies as the readiest and most natural translation of the principle of equal opportunity, democratic peoples had actually developed a pride of gain and openly worked for the sake of material advantage.[46] In every ordered society "wealth is a sacred thing," says Anatole France in *Penguin Island;* "in a democracy it is the only sacred thing. . . ." [47]

In discussing the pride of gain inherent in "democratic" man, de Tocqueville remarked that this was in contradiction to the concept of aristocratic honor which was marked by a contempt of profit as a reward for social service. De Tocqueville realized, of course, that this opposition was often only a public ideal, for aristocrats actually permitted high and low motivations to intermingle "in the depths of their souls." The distinction is important ideologically, however, as a means of understanding the anxious and devoted forms of self-cultivation practiced by literary elites. For it is a fundamental characteristic of the gentleman of the mind, as compared to the mere social gentleman, that the former, having no title of excellence other than his own inner virtues, cannot allow himself subjective ambiguities and must pledge himself to an absolute and indeed notorious canon of aristocratic behavior. The point will be seen if we place next to Baudelaire's Dandy a literary example of the businessman such as the Josiah Bounderby of Charles Dickens'

Hard Times. Bounderby is the incarnation of naked business success—a banker, merchant, and manufacturer with the loud and brutal self-reliance of one who has triumphed over low and sweaty beginnings. His early poverty, from which there was no escape but power, is a source not of shame but of pride. The Dandy, on the other hand, is not only necessarily well-off, but also unaccountably so; his is a "natural" state of leisure which allows him to turn his person into a finely-worked-out collection of spiritual detail resting on a modulated balance of circumspection, diffidence, and lofty self-esteem. The Dandy stood, Baudelaire said, for the "majestic modesty" of the man of letters. Bounderby, according to Dickens, was a "bully of humility." One speaks for the distance and composure of "inherent" values, the other for the plain but muscular pride of the pragmatic. It is Bounderby who says at one point:

I am a Coketown man. I am Josiah Bounderby of Coketown. I know the bricks of this town, and I know the works of this town, and I know the chimneys of this town . . . and I know the Hands of this town. When a man tells me anything about imaginative qualities, I always tell that man . . . that I know what he means. He means turtle-soup and venison, with a gold spoon, and that he wants to be set up with a coach and six.[48]

"Persons of any condition are authorized to make window panes," wrote a French intendant in 1700, "as distinguished from artistic glass which is reserved for gentle folk." [49] It is under the weight of such a tradition that Dickens could perceive the implicit link between intellectual versions of the claims and postures of traditional high status and the language of literary complaints. This and the seriousness with which Baudelaire and Flaubert argued the relationship between spirituality and elegance, reveals the vacuum left in Western society by the passing of an aristocracy capable of embracing within one class not only grace and elegance but also splendor and power. It exposes, too, the strain inevitable in creating an aristocracy based solely on cultural exertion, on "the heavenly gifts which neither labor nor money can confer."

According to Max Weber, the principal task of the Chinese mandarin was to make his person a flawless mirror of his inward harmony because on this alone rested his claim to public esteem and his right to hold public power.[50] Flaubert, in writing about his mandarin, suggested that he, too, conceived this figure as the vehicle of a self-conscious and ritually demanding discipline. And such was, of course, the intent and image of the Baudelairian Dandy. Having thus made the deliberate *symbolic* decision to stand for aristocratic values, the literary elite of the nineteenth century had no choice but to bend every intellectual and psychological passion to the denial of utility. However, considering the social and economic circumstances of their times, they were faced with some inescapable paradoxical prospects. Baudelaire's aristocracy was conceived as a moral and aesthetic gesture against money, a restoration of the spiritual side of honorific leisure at a time when the traditional property basis of that leisure—land, rents, and courtly favors—no longer existed and could not, therefore, provide the intellectual with material support. Indeed, when it came to the source of subsistence for the new aristocracy, Baudelaire could at best only hide the realities of the modern market, and his description of the Dandy as one who is rich but does not work is but an illusion permitting money to flow mysteriously into the Dandy's pocket. Flaubert, too, confronted the problem of how to profit from the market while avoiding spiritual pollution, but his prescription was something more than a verbal utopia. Whereas in the past, one class had provided material services and another cultivated values, a resourceful modern intellectual might attempt to embrace both functions within one individual. He should take care, however, to keep the management of property from infecting his mind and imagination. A successful man of letters, Flaubert said, would "live like a bourgeois but think as a demigod." [51]

Baudelaire's fantasy of a lifetime of unlimited credit appears to coincide in part with George Bernard Shaw's description of the relations between society and the gentleman. The gentleman, according to Shaw, is an individual who tells himself: "I want to be a cultured human being; I want to live in the fullest sense; I require a generous subsistence . . . and I expect my country to organize itself in such a way as to secure me that." But Shaw adds that the true gentleman also says: "In return I am willing to give my country the best service of which I am capable." [52] The Baudelairian Dandy, to the contrary, meets his obligations by his mere existence and presence, by providing the spectacle of the cultural prince as a self-justifying event; this theory inevitably provides the excuse for the figure of the sensitive soul as a confidence man such as one finds, for one example, in Thomas Mann's *Felix Krull*.[53] As for the Flaubertian coexistence of art and business within separate compartments of the soul, its best example may, perhaps, be found in the wedding of capitalistic skills and intellectual gifts with which Benjamin Disraeli endowed the character of Sidonia in his novel *Coningsby*. The head of "the world's most powerful banking family" and a man able to pay the interest on the English national debt out of his own pocket, Sidonia is also the prototype of the unorthodox intellectual aristocrat—a kaleidoscopic and opulent world-Bohemian who befriends authors, artists, philosophers, gypsies, and Carbonari, who is at home in Paris, Naples, Africa or Brazil and whose wizard mind had mastered "all the sources of human knowledge . . . the learning of every nation, and all the tongues dead or living, of every literature, Western and Oriental." [54]

The discipline of Dandyism and the techniques it devised to present itself before the world have, for better or for worse, become a part of the modern literary manner. According to the methodical hero of Edgar Allan Poe's *The Businessman,* only the common person was capable of discharging routinary obligations—never the *outré*. Conversely, to make of the *outré* a daily task and display was precisely the point of Baudelaire's literary-aristocratic model. Max Weber's representative of the ethical revolution in the modern market place had been the Puritan, the "earthly ascetic" whose morally uplifting energies could be transformed into economic results. Baudelaire's Dandy is also such a "typical ideal" figure, but one who dreams of an aesthetic asceticism in which all impulses are directed toward artistic craftsmanship and all dedication to the perfection of the personality alone. It is as part of this modern tradition that one can understand the morality of Tennessee Williams' immeasurably refined poet, in *Suddenly Last Summer,* whose ethical fiber lay in his strength to surrender the pleasures of the table so that he would remain slender and youthful forever.[55] It is also within such a tradition that we can understand André Gide's Lafcadio, who practiced originality as Pascal beseeched salvation. Pascal stabbed himself with a pin when he was guilty of sinful thoughts; Lafcadio used a similar method as penance for commonplace ideas.[56]

In his recent book *The Two Cultures,* Sir Charles P. Snow expressed concern with the unrest and homelessness of literary men which, he says, not only creates an awkward rift within Western civilization but represents an actual danger to its survival. The problem, Snow says, is that the soulful alarm displayed by literary intellectuals in the face of the modern world—an attitude which now extends from the Left Bank to Chelsea, Oxford, Greenwich Village, and the America campus —represents really nothing more than the irrational refusal to accept the scientific and technological revolution of the last two centuries. To the customary gestures of recoil from "cheap, naïve optimism and materialism" Snow answers that "materialism," properly understood, not only has not made scientists— the presumed chief protagonists of it—any less human, but in fact, is looked upon by the majority of the people in this world as a blessing, not a disgrace. Most men of science, he says, have a sense of the personal predicament of man, even a tragic sense of it. They know that much in life is disappointing and solitary. But they see no reason why, if the human condition is tragic, the social condition should also be so. Nor do they understand why writers and artists should think of industrialization—the creature of materialism, science, technology, and so forth—as a horror when it is the only hope of poor societies to escape their poverty, as such societies prove by industrializing as soon as they can.[57]

Even though industrialization has sometimes brought painful immediate problems, what Snow says about the desire for it in economically stationary societies is, of course, undoubtedly true. Yet, to maintain that the literary repugnance for science, technology, and manufacturing is a kind of social "treason" (as Snow has been known to maintain) is far from providing us with an explanation for these questionable intellectual dispositions. Indeed, the book not only fails to offer such an explanation but part of the way along leaves the question behind altogether. Instead, Snow offers a general warning about the political dangers of neglecting scientific training in a world where the direction of imminent social change is bound to fall into the hands of those who can provide the scientific and technological fulfillment of revolutionary dreams.

Snow regards the politics of some modern writers—Yeats, Lawrence, and Eliot among them—as "silly when not wicked." But why should this be so? Why should a society deliberately setting out to attain a happier material life make the literary mind depressed? After all, as Snow remarks, artists, writers, and scientists generally belong to the same class, the middle class, and they have, therefore, nothing to lose socially from mass well-being. If, as Snows says, scientists have a common way of looking at the world and a way of speaking about it, could it not be that the literary problem is related to an intellectual language and a style which also reflect a common image of the world?

Literary men are frequently ignorant of the rudiments of

modern science, and their easygoing dismissal of scientific discoveries as trivial is regarded by Snow, quite correctly, as something of a polite scandal. At the same time, Snow believes that scientists should be better read and more sensitive to the concerns of the humanistic mind. Such peacemaking suggestions are no doubt likely to induce decorum and amiability at the intellectual dinner table. They are not, on the other hand, likely to solve the problem inasmuch as they have very little to do with it. What one must understand is that the strange sense of oppressiveness, shown by poets, novelists, and artists in the face of scientific precision and rigor, and other manifestations of rationalized purpose, comes from profound differences in the concept and the feeling of intellectual freedom as it is experienced by the aesthetic and literary mind when compared with the rational scientific mind. To the scientist, unfreedom and constraint are represented by the inability to solve a specific problem. In literature, on the contrary, a sense of intellectual foreclosure, of the end of the imagination's ability to move, to inspect, and to consider, is produced by the possibility of solving the problem. Literature, in other words, is simply a different kind of knowledge. It can be a profound index of social reality. But its magnitude as art or as document does not as a rule depend on its capacity to solve problems in the scientific sense. It would be the height of idiosyncratic antiquarianism for a physicist to ask his pupils to base their training on a mastery of Aristotle or on seventeenth-century texts. But if the same standards were applied to English departments large portions of them would have to be disbanded. In literary art the opportunity for intellectual exertion, curiosity, struggle—in a word, freedom—depends on the possibility of returning to the human predicament, on the assumption that human problems are in some sense insoluble, just as the moral and aesthetic imagination is in some sense inexhaustible.

In social relations, too, and for the same reason, the literary mind has rejected the scientific aspiration to control human reality in unambiguous terms. Sociologists such as Max Weber have regarded "calculability," the smooth and predictable discharge of explicit administrative, legal, and economic functions, as an inevitable development of modern institutions and, indeed, their essential feature. Such calculability, Weber said, depended on the social triumph of the principles of bureaucratic rule, on clear relationships between specific ends and specific means, and on the elimination from institutional activity of all "unreasonable," that is, subjective, motivations.[58] Weber looked upon this process as desirable in many ways. It provided the foundations of an efficient system of public services. It undermined privilege and the influence of kinship and favor in the conduct of public affairs. He was, nevertheless, repelled by and even vaguely afraid of the human type that modern bureaucracies needed for their operation—the men of narrow aspirations, of small, airless minds living by legalistic snobbery; "the Puritan willed to be the vocational man." [59]

The literary man was, of course, equally repelled and alarmed, but he extended his concern beyond the bureaucrat to the whole of the modern social climate. He perceived, for example, that while all systems of political rule must attempt to guide and determine human destinies, none did so with such deliberate regularity and such appetite for manipulation as the rationalized social order. Edward Shils has remarked that governments in the past were able to count on the traditionalism of the governed—that is, on their acceptance of an immemorial social predicament—as the basis on which power was exercised. In modern societies, on the contrary, rulers invited novel expectations on the part of their subjects and made their bid for power on the ability to fulfill these expectations. In other words, modern political power rested on the stimulation of mass hopes and on the mass approval which followed mass gratification. Shils also noticed that the kinds of social aspirations first promoted and then adopted as political programs by modern regimes are most frequently those whose benefits can be counted, measured, and explicitly distributed: technological advance, high economic productivity, general material welfare, and a system of education designed to increase the share of the general population in technical, professional, and bureaucratic opportunities; eventually, of course, such an educational system and the occupations and professions it stimulated would service the social enterprises advocated by the political state.[60] * It was a central theme of de Tocqueville's famous study of democracy that there was a connection between modern equalitarianism and a pragmatic and materialistic social climate. Taking this loosely, modern governments may be generally regarded as democratic in the sense that they are pledged to advance the interests of the masses. There is, however, an important difference between de Tocqueville's classical account of the psychology of equalitarian democracy and Shils' analysis of mass-oriented governments. What de Tocqueville saw was a spontaneous taste for material gratification on the part of the equalitarian man. What Shils wishes to point out is that modern political organization is conceived as a device for the continuous solution of social problems and that, because of this, these problems are themselves conceived in such a way as to make them amenable to explicit and general solutions in the bureaucratic style. Therefore, popular governments and efficiency-seeking societies will constantly press men toward larger-scale and more simplified realms of social and personal experience.

Now, whether one regards modern literary despair as egotistical or merely wasteful, one cannot easily deny its sociological interest. The convergence of mass tendencies, institutional

* This may seem to apply only to heavily "socialized" political and economic systems. However, even in representative democracies and so-called free economies there has been an enormous increase in the number of social services performed by the political institutions, the growth of the political bureaucracy as a profession, and in the public regulation of private enterprise. Furthermore, because of its size and complexity, privately owned enterprise takes on some of the features, limitations, and responsibilities of semi-public services and bureaucracies.

rationalization, and what may be called political scientism are
distinct features of the modern world. In passionately rejecting these developments, literary men were not only speaking
for their own tastes and antipathies. They were also expressing
—indeed, they were among the first to express—the fear, peculiar to our society, that ever more successful instruments of public welfare may, paradoxically, represent a threat to the survival
of traditional ways of individualized existence. Such a fear may
be rational or irrational, justified or unjustified, responsible
or irresponsible, but one cannot deny that it has become a
fairly general form of social disquiet and not merely an item of
literary sensibility.

Conversely, the social perceptions of modern literature serve
to explain why that literature has celebrated the intimate and
the excessive, self-cultivation and self-expression, haughty in-
tellectualism and the aesthetics of life-playing, heroes of arrogance and heroes of despair, sensitive men and ironic failures.
Nietzsche, Hemingway, Stendhal, Dostoevsky, and Scott Fitz-
gerald are all understandable within the spirit of this literature.
But so is the obscure nonhero of George Orwell's *Nineteen
Eighty Four,* a book whose very title has become almost an intellectual slogan in our day. Orwell was nurtured on a number
of left-wing causes. He later became a disappointed commenta-
tor on the politics of his time and *Nineteen Eighty Four,* his
last novel, is commonly taken as an attack on political totalitarianism. It is this, but it is also a morality tale intended to por-
tray the conflict between a personal way of life and certain inherent tendencies of modern public organization when these are
carried to their ultimate fulfillment. The nightmare of living under an insatiably dogmatic political system armed with absolute means of repression is, of course, there. But there is, in addition an awareness of other conflicts which reflect not only the
political but also the "human" implacability of modern public
power and efficiency. Winston Smith, the protagonist of Orwell's novel, is drawn like Baudelaire's poet to frail and useless

things which seem to offer him a respite from the inescapable purposefulness and single-mindedness of his surroundings; the destruction of ancient buildings inexplicably saddens him, and he has a curious passion for second-hand stores and old fashioned gimcracks like glass paperweights adorned with inlaid flowers. Winston's ultimate doom, however, follows his attempt to satisfy the most profound of all personal needs (somehow still alive within the modern social robot), love. This the state and party will not tolerate, and it is only after Winston wills the destruction of personal love that his political illumination and his membership in the new order become final and complete. Indeed, Orwell would seem to have placed Weber's vision of love as the great enemy of modern "rationality" in the cruelest of perspectives. *Nineteen Eighty Four* not only tells us that love represents the ultimate withdrawal from public demands, it also forecasts the obliteration of love at the hands of a state which will not allow the survival of this last shelter from nonpublic purpose.[61]

The techniques developed by literary rebels as a means of avoiding cultural equalization in an age they regard as dominated by uniformity change from time to time, yet they tend to remain close in spirit. In their day, Flaubert and Baudelaire met the appearance of a well-dressed populace by inventing a new personal elegance. In our day, when "style" is being distributed on the mass market, such people as the American "beats" have chosen the "new poverty," the elitism of nonconsumption. There is also the issue of preventing the loss of aesthetic surprise in an environment swamped by utilitarianism and oversocialized piousness. One traditional response to this was provided by the outrageous idiosyncrasies and cryptic styles of willfulness invented by the nineteenth-century Bohemians and still practiced by their heirs.* Another is the literary enthusiasm for happenings whose sole value resides in a mo-

* It would be hard to conceive of an intellectual epoch other than our own in which one would be expected to see the point of the "explana-

ment of great poignancy or in a display of memorable singularity. Thus, for example, Hemingway explained that the boredom of a poor bullfight might be relieved by looking closely at
the bullfighter's face. One could then see his fear and *that* was
interesting. Baudelaire, we recall, thought that though Latin-
American politics were barbarous, at least they caused people
to kill each other, just as the only form of political activity of
interest to Flaubert was the riot, that is, the failure of politics.
Such remarks may be regarded as being themselves as picturesque and irresponsible as the things they intended to praise.
Yet even Bertrand Russell, a man who has dedicated his life to
the support of the scientific method (and Snow might have noted
this) has recently become fearful of some of the consequences
of an excessively rationalized society. He goes as far as to say
that the rule of the "administrative type" at the service of efficiency for its own sake is the greatest of our present dangers
outside of atomic destruction.[62] Indeed, it is possible to discover
in modern literature not only a rejection of efficiency but, in
fact, a positive attachment to failure. There is reverent pity
for the sensitive victim of mechanized existence, just as there is
delight at the spectacle of the machinery of the modern world
falling flat on its face. One can hear the joy and relief of a
writer like Honor Tracy as she enters Spain, a country yet un-
blighted by modernity, and realizes at once that bathrooms can
now be expected to behave comically, that nobody is likely to
obey rules, and that public services are a charade of infuriating
but colorful confusion.[63] If philistines are upset by late trains or
poor plumbing, a whole minor literary genre has grown in our
day dedicated to the praise of societies where technological efficiency may be low, but human excitement is high.

The champions of "personalization" in an "age of imper-

---

tion" given by the Spanish novelist Ramón del Valle Inclán for his taking
a trip to Mexico; it was, he said, the only country with an "X" in its
name.

sonality" have appealed to many things—the worship of art over routine, of pleasure over discipline, of the individual over the community—and they have done so with passion and defiance as well as anxiety and distress. However, Weber's large views on social rationality, Shils' observations on modern populism, the black utopias of Orwell and others, and the history of political disappointment of many figures of contemporary letters all point to a sense of inescapable and near desperate predicament caused by the thought that the problems of individualism and creative and emotional free play may occur under all of the political and economic dispensations of the modern age. The first reaction and the earlier attack was, of course, against the middle class. Scholars, particularly present-day sociologists, may argue about what the middle class means as a term or as a reality. But one finds little ambiguity when one deals with the middle class not as a socioeconomic entity but as a system of values, and especially as a system of values observed by literary men.* Contemporary sociologists

* Some European sociologists seem to have a fairly clear notion of where one class begins and another ends, and even of the social and economic provinces within one class. Lewis and Maude, writing of the English middle class, contrast the white-collar families of the turn of the century, languishing below the "public" school circuit in a suburban proliferation of "Acacia Villas," with the high-bourgeois gentlemen of Arnold Bennett's recollections, men of "assured curt voices and proud carriage," who belonged to a caste "completely free from the cares which beset at least five-sixths of the English nation." On the other hand, a uniformity of terms does not always accompany such careful distinctions. Some French sociologists use the expression "middle class" to refer to an essentially provincial world of small businessmen and small-town civil servants and professionals. Others put the middle class between the upper class (consisting of large-scale industrialists, the professional elite and great state functionaries) on the one side, and manual and white-collar workers on the other. In America two famous surveys which are now part of the sociological folklore showed that between 79 per cent and 88 per cent of Americans regarded themselves as members of the middle class. Later studies by Richard Centers disputed these findings, and later still the several volumes by W. Lloyd Warner and his associates offered a precise classification of the American social order. Yet, for all of these

have said that one of the differences between the lower and
the middle classes is that the first lives for "short-run hedonism" and the second is capable of "delayed gratification," that
is to say, of denying itself immediate pleasure and, as a consequence, of accumulating the economic resources needed for its
eventual social improvement. This distinction is only the most
recent contribution to the history of portrayals of the middle
class and actually rests on a reiteration of Max Weber's thesis
and the preachments of a long line of middle-class moralists
like Daniel Defoe, who in 1745 wrote: "I cannot allow any
pleasures to be innocent when they turn away either the body or
the mind of the tradesman from one needful thing which his calling makes necessary: I mean the application of both his head and
his hand to his business." [64] Still, it does serve to remind us that,
if one side of the literary reaction against the middle class has
been the spirit of the mandarinate—the discretion and loftiness
of the self-created intellectual aristocrat before the money-and-
tools secularity of the businessman—another side was the championing of the street-corner folk, the Bohemians, and even the

---

clarifications and additions, a sense of evasiveness persists. In his recent
Class in American Society, Leonard Riessman points out that because
of a belief in social equality, class in the United States tends to mean
caste. He also finds that, according to "Hometown," his model sample,
"the number of classes that may be recognized varies depending on the
number of social differences the Hometowners can detect and agree
upon." Seymour Lipset and Reinhard Bendix, in an abundantly documented study, maintain that in fact there is no substantial difference in
the fluidity and mobility of American and European societies, and that
the appearance that America is more mobile has to do with the style of
manners and the means of acquiring and exhibiting social symbols in the
United States. W. Lloyd Warner & Paul S. Lunt, *The Social Life of a
Modern Community* (New Haven: Yale University Press, 1941); W.
Lloyd Warner & Associates, *Democracy in Jonesville* (New York: Harper
& Bros., 1949); Ruth Rosner Kornhauser, "The Warner Approach to
Social Stratification," in Reinhard Bendix & Seymour Martin Lipset,
Class, Status and Power (Glencoe, Ill.: The Free Press, 1953); Leonard
Riessman, *Class in American Society* (Glencoe, Ill.: The Free Press,
1960); Seymour Martin Lipset & Reinhard Bendix, *Social Mobility and
Industrial Society* (Berkeley: University of California Press, 1959).

derelicts, or in other words all the practitioners of the ancient and spontaneous art of "short-run hedonism." The prudence and prudery of the middle classes may look with horror upon lust, waste, irresponsibility, superstition, and violence, and middle-class "reform" may seek to eradicate them from society as a whole. But for the literary imagination these traits are often the companions of amusement, charm, grace, courage, and the daily predicament of human triumph and failure and, within failure, survival, a spectacle always reassuring to those bored with the hygienic and relentless optimism of the present age.

Now if, as Gustave Flaubert said, the great revolution of our time was the conquest of modern society by the spirit of the middle class, intellectuals might have found consolation and, presumably, the solution of their problems in the victory of Marxist political forces in Russia and elsewhere. And it is true, of course, that many writers and artists of the last two generations chose for a time to look upon the Soviet Union as the very instrument of their salvation. This, however, was followed by a painful though protracted collapse of such illusions, not only among the distinguished and the important, but also among the obscure members of the intellectual rank and file. Of some of the Americans of the "Beat Generation," Lawrence Lipton has said:

We felt that all the Bolsheviks had succeeded in absorbing so far were the headaches of the ruling class, the manufacture of things, the production and distribution of problems, the bookkeeping that went with it. We were expropriating the things of inner gratification and lasting value, and we were doing it without overthrowing the rich.[65]

As a weary dismissal of all things not of "lasting value" or capable of producing "inner gratification," Lipton's statement may appear as one more echo of the pained and supercilious soulfulness of the romantic inheritance. But the tone is above all Stendhalian: the Bolsheviks are now the new bourgeoisie, the new managers of that "collection of ugly details" which, according to Stendhal, constituted the great concern of the middle class. In Baudelaire's words we might say that nothing much had happened other than the emergence of a new generation of work horses in the stables of mankind.

When Max Weber spoke of the dictates and powers of modern social rationalism, he had in mind the emergence of the great national bureaucracies and industrial and financial combines of recent history, and he saw no sign of retreat in the growth of either political or economic rationalism. Marx, on the other hand, while attempting to bring about a rational revolution in the social structure of mankind, promised nevertheless that state institutions would dissolve because the individual himself would become the carrier of an universal rationality. Everyone knows that "the withering away of the state" has yet to approach its beginnings in the Soviet Union nearly half a century after the revolution. Some contemporary literary attacks on Soviet reality, however, complain not so much of the failure of social rationality to emerge but of the excess of rationality which already exists. There are in Soviet literature, too, nonheroes whose human sentiments are unable to withstand the tide of modern collective morality. One such is the would-be production manager in Yuri Olesha's *The Wayward Comrade,* whose downfall is brought about by his attachment to archaic feelings—vanity, jealousy, honor—such as no bureaucracy would tolerate, the "old" feelings "glorified by poets" which still haunt him and of which he would like to organize a "final parade." [66] D. H. Lawrence may have spoken for non-Marxists and post-Marxists when he said that all of modern society was "a steady sort of Bolshevism; just killing the human thing and worshiping the mechanical thing." [67]

The problem of a scientific versus a literary culture reaches, therefore, into much more intractable areas than those suggested by Sir Charles P. Snow. It is not merely a question of a vain and superstitious disregard for science or the provincialism

209

of humanists who refuse to accept the enormous managerial problems of the modern world, or of the willful social obscurantism of the romantic mind. It is a question of the essential impact of an ever more rationalized mode of existence upon the life-space available to some of the oldest forms of human imagination. If a scientifically intended society means putting human experience on a flat, well-lit plane which leads in a straight line toward a perennially deliberate future, the literary mind may be said to represent in its most rebellious form a case of intellectual fatigue before the secular version of infinity.

NOTES TO PART THREE

1. Émile Durkheim, *The Social Division of Labor* (Glencoe, Ill.: The Free Press, 1949), p. 3.
2. Isaac Disraeli, *The Literary Character of Men of Genius* (London: Frederick Warner & Co.), p. 15.
3. Sister Catherine Theresa Rapp, "Burgher and Peasant in the Works of Thomasin von Zilcaria, Freidank and Hugo von Trimberg," *The Catholic University of America Studies in German*, VII, 91-92.
4. Cited in Louis B. Wright, *op. cit.*, p. 24.
5. Roy Lewis & Angus Maude, *The English Middle Classes* (London: Phoenix House, 1949), pp. 22-23, 41-42.
6. Veblen, *The Theory of the Leisure Class*, Chs. I, II.
7. *Ibid.*, p. 48.
8. W. H. Auden, "The Dyer's Hand," *The Anchor Review*, II, (Garden City, New York: Doubleday Anchor Books, 1957), pp. 255-256.
9. Alfred Kazin, *On Native Grounds* (New York: Reynal Hitchcock, 1942), p. 312.
10. Sigmund Freud, *Civilization and Its Discontents* (London: The Hogarth Press, 1949), p. 73; see also: "Civilized Sexual Morality and Modern Nervousness," *Collected Papers* (5 vols.; London: The Hogarth Press, 1934), II, 76-99.
11. Honoré de Balzac, *La Comédie humaine* (53 vols.; Philadelphia: George Barrie and Son, 1897), XVII, 285.
12. Stendhal, *Mélanges de littérature*, II, 127.
13. Baudelaire, *Oeuvres complètes*, VI, 95.
14. D. H. Lawrence, *Studies in Classical American Literature* (Garden City, New York: Doubleday Anchor Books, 1955), p. 20.

15. D. H. Lawrence, *A Propos Lady Chatterley's Lover* (London: Mandrake Press Ltd., 1930), pp. 25-30.

16. D. H. Lawrence, *Lady Chatterley's Lover* (New York: The American Library, 1959), pp. 142-143.

17. *Ibid.,* p. 142.

18. Lawrence, *A Propos Lady Chatterley's Lover,* p. 59.

19. Arthur Miller, *Death of a Salesman* (New York: Viking Press, 1949).

20. Émile Durkheim, *Suicide,* trans. John A. Spaulding & George Simpson (Glencoe, Ill.: The Free Press, 1951), p. 213.

21. D. H. Lawrence, *The Plumed Serpent* (New York: Vintage Books, 1959), p. 143.

22. John Steinbeck, *Tortilla Flat* (New York: Grosset & Dunlap, 1935); William Saroyan, *My Name Is Aram* (New York: Harcourt, Brace & Co., 1940); Du Bose Heyward, *Porgy* (New York: George H. Doran, 1925); Moss Hart & George S. Kaufmann, *You Can't Take It with You* (New York-Toronto: Farrar & Rinehart, 1937), p. 3.

23. Norman Mailer, *The White Negro* (San Francisco: City Lights Books), pp. 33 ff.

24. Jack Kerouac, *On the Road* (New York: New American Library, 1958), pp. 148-149.

25. Lawrence Lipton, *The Holy Barbarians* (New York: Julian Messner, Inc., 1959).

26. Flaubert, *Selected Letters,* pp. 23, 33, 39, 77, 159, 171, 177.

27. Norman Mailer, *Advertisements for Myself* (New York: Signet Books, 1960), pp. 379-380.

28. Sigmund Freud, "The Origins and Development of Psychoanalysis," in *General Selections from the Works of Sigmund Freud,* ed. John Rickman (Garden City, New York: Anchor Books, 1957).

29. See, for example: "Character and Anal Eroticism," *Collected Papers,* **II,** 45-50.

30. Vandam, *op. cit.,* **I,** 239.

31. *From Max Weber: Essays in Sociology,* eds. Hans Gerth & C. Wright Mills (New York: Galaxy Books, 1958), pp. 196 ff. For a discussion of Weber's concept of ideas as historical causes see: Reinhard Bendix, *Max Weber: An Intellectual Portrait* (New York: Doubleday & Co., 1960), pp. 85ff. For a general analysis of Weber's concept of bureaucracy see: *Ibid.,* pp. 48ff.

32. Thorstein Veblen, *The Theory of Business Enterprise* (New York: Mentor Books, 1958), Chap. II, IX

33. Marx & Engels, *Communist Manifesto,* pp. 128-129.

34. John Stuart Mill, *On Liberty,* ed. Alburey Castell (New York: Appleton-Croft, Inc., 1947), pp. 60-62.

35. *Ibid.,* p. 61.

36. *Loc. cit.*

37. *Ibid.,* p. 59.

38. Cited in Raymond Williams, *Culture and Society* (Garden City, New York: Anchor Books, 1960), p. 55.

39. Lewis & Maude, *op. cit.,* p. 42.

40. Voltaire, *Works,* **XXIII**, 257-258.

41. *History of Western Civilization: Selected Readings* (9 vols.; Chicago: The University Press, 1960), **IX**, 26.

42. Cited in *ibid.,* **VIII**, 135-136.

43. *From Max Weber: Essays in Sociology,* p. 347.

44. Cited in *History of Western Civilization: Selected Readings,* **VIII**, 53.

45. Emanuel Sieyès, *Qu'est-ce que c'est le tiers état?* (Paris: Société de l'histoire de la Revolution Française, 1888), p. 28.

46. De Tocqueville, *Democracy in America,* **II**, 152.

47. Anatole France, *Penguin Island,* trans. A. W. Evans (London: John Lane, The Bodley Head, Ltd., 1927), p. 203.

48. Charles Dickens, *Hard Times* (2 vols.; New York: Sheldon & Co., 1863), **I**, 316.

49. John U. Neff, *Cultural Foundations of Industrial Society* (New York: Harper & Brothers Torchbooks, 1958), p. 52.

50. *From Max Weber: Essays in Sociology,* p. 436.

51. Cited in Spencer, *op. cit.,* p. 118.

52. Cited in Eric Bentley, *Bernard Shaw* (New York: New Directions Paperbacks, 1957), pp. 35-36.

53. Thomas Mann, *The Confessions of Felix Krull, Confidence Man,* trans. Denver Lindley (New York: Alfred A. Knopf, 1955).

54. Benjamin Disraeli (Earl Beaconsfield), *Coningsby* (London: J. M. Dent Sons & Co.), pp. 177-180.

55. Edgar Allan Poe, *Works* (4 vols.; London: A. and C. Black, 1913), **II**, 560; Tennessee Williams, *Suddenly Last Summer* (New York: New Directions, 1958).

56. André Gide, *Lafcadio's Adventures,* trans. Dorothy Bussy (New York: Alfred A. Knopf, 1951).

57. C. P. Snow, *The Two Cultures* (New York: Cambridge University Press, 1959).

58. *From Max Weber: Essays in Sociology,* p. 293.

59. *Ibid.,* p. 50.

60. Edward Shils, "Political Developments in the New States," *Comparative Studies in Society and History,* **II**, No. 3, April 1960, pp. 265 ff.

61. George Orwell, *Nineteen Eighty Four* (New York: Harcourt Brace, 1949).

62. *Bertrand Russell Speaks His Mind* (New York: Bard Books, 1960), pp. 137 ff.

63. Honor Tracy, *Silk Hats and No Breakfast* (New York: Random House, 1958).

64. Daniel Defoe, *The Complete English Tradesman* (London: J. Rivington, 1745), p. 66.

65. Lipton, *op. cit.*, p. 147.

66. Yurii Olesha, *The Wayward Comrade and the Commissars,* trans. Andrew R. MacAndrew (New York: Signet Books, 1960), pp. 76-77.

67. Lewis & Maude, *op. cit.*, p. 56.

INDEX